IF FOUND PLEASE RETURN TO

- -

Name
- -

Address
- -

- -

- -

- -

This book saved my bacon

The Author in Fancy Dress as a Side of Bacon, designed by himself, which took the First Prize of Forty Guineas at the Covent Garden Fancy Dress Ball, April 1894.

In 2007, two east London-born brothers in their early twenties, Chris O'Connor and James Brundle, transformed a rundown off-licence called Paul's Wines in Walthamstow Village into an award-winning, world-class convenience store and restaurant concept named Eat 17 in honour of their local postcode. Smoky-sweet Bacon Jam was created in the Walthamstow kitchen to top Eat 17's famous burgers. After it received national attention on the *Jonathan Ross Show* and *QI* (bacon + jam? wtf?), Bacon Jam's popularity exploded. By the time the *Guardian* called it 'arguably [Walthamstow's] most unlikely and successful export', this pink-pig-packaged, cult condiment was available nationwide in supermarkets from Tesco to Sainsbury's, as well as at hundreds of quality independents throughout the UK and beyond.

eat¹⁷ THE BACON JAM COOKBOOK

IT'S A PROPER PIG-OUT

ROBINSON

ROBINSON

First published in 2016 by
Robinson

1 3 5 7 9 10 8 6 4 2

Selection and Introduction
Copyright © Pretext Limited,
2016

Typeset in Sentinel and
designed by Andrew Barron
@ thextension

Printed and bound in China

Robinson
An imprint of
Little, Brown Book Group
Carmelite House
50 Victoria Embankment
London EC4Y 0DZ

An Hachette UK Company
www.hachette.co.uk

www.littlebrown.co.uk

A CIP catalogue record for
this book is available from the
British Library.

ISBN: 978-1-47213-724-1

Warning!

This book is not for vegetarians. It's not for vegans either. It's probably unlikely that either would enjoy anything about this book. We just want to apologise for this. In advance. Because we at Eat 17 love vegetarians – vegans too. We carry lots of vegetarian and vegan products in our east London shops, and we're pretty sure that we get lots of vegetarians and vegans shopping at Eat 17 (at least we hope so). Eat 17 loves vegetarians. Vegans too. We really do. But...

... you see, this book... is a book about BACON, the love of bacon, adding more bacon, spreadable bacon, bacon, bacon, bacon and making the world just a little bit more of a baconier, meatier place.

So, again, before we even start: apologies from Eat 17. To the vegetarians and the vegans of this world: we love you. But maybe you should put this book down now and back away slowly. Because this book probably isn't for you.

Sincerely
Eat 17

Contents

Why Bacon Jam?

Everyone knows that more bacon means happier food and, by extension, creates more happiness in the world so that's why Eat 17's iconic pink jar screams **Happiness** to a vast majority of bacon lovers throughout the UK. Bacon Jam is basically spreadable happiness. It allows you to bacon-ify anything. Burgers? Meat them up with a smear of Bacon Jam. Grilled cheese? A quick spoonful of bacon is all it takes. No longer is a frying pan required to put a smile on your face. Serenity and contentment is just one small pink jar away. You can even ruin/ SAVE perfectly acceptable vegetarian food with the tasty goodness of bacon.

2 If bacon is wrong, I don't want to be right. Make food happy, give it bacon. Do it.

According to the British Sandwich Association, more than 7,000 tonnes of bacon is used in ready-made sandwiches sold in the UK every year. The dramatically titled pork-monitoring survey, Porkwatch, also wants us to know that we spent £954.3 million buying bacon to cook at home in 2015. That's 155,600 tonnes of bacon. And one-third of that was solely dedicated to bacon sandwiches. Now that's a lot of bacon.

And if you do an internet search on the word 'bacon', you'll be bombarded with the special form of meat worship that can only be devoted to bacon. There's bacon toothpaste, plasters, soap, mints, candles, soda, cologne, lube (*ew*), you name it, someone somewhere has tried to make it smell, taste or look like bacon.

Now this is either a huge conspiracy perpetuated by the pork belly industry or people really do love this stuff. It seems that the vast majority of the population may have succumbed to the captivating allure of tasty, crispy bacon.

So there. That's why Bacon Jam.

The Americans certainly love their bacon. *Left*: Drink the pain away with drinkable bacon from Jones Soda; *right, top*: Make yourself irresistable by showering with bacon-scented soap from Outlaw Soaps;

near right: Heal all wounds with the magic poultice that is Archie McPhee's bacon bandage; *far right*: You'll be a guaranteed hit at the kissing booth after a quick brush with some bacon toothpaste.

4   Bacon + Jam @ Eat 17

'This isn't a Soho delicatessen – it's a Spar shop in unglamorous Walthamstow, north-east London, whose owners have gone even further by creating what is arguably the area's most unlikely and successful export: Bacon Jam. Recently name-checked by Stephen Fry on BBC2 show QI*...'*

Guardian, September 2012

It seemed obvious to write a cookbook about how to use Bacon Jam.

People were perplexed to start with. Bacon + jam? It seemed as though nobody could wrap their heads around it. Jonathan Ross couldn't. Neither could actress, Sarah Jessica Parker when she tried some on his talk show in 2011 (although, to be fair, she gave it a good shot).

Was it sweet? Savoury? Where were you supposed to put it? Just a little or a lot? Was it only for breakfast? Or was it an ingredient? Had the world of jam gone totally crazy?

There was a lot of gnashing of teeth about BACON and JAM, these two words that had once been considered perfectly acceptable all on their own. Did they belong together? Who had caused this fusion? Was it right and proper? Should it be stopped?

To this day, we're not really sure what Stephen Fry thought, one way or the other, when he mentioned us on *QI*. He seemed as bemused as always so it was hard to tell.

Once the press started weighing in, well, things just snowballed from there. There was loads of positive feedback, writers falling in love with this strange combo of bacon + jam, kudos from right and left.

Our spreadable bacon happiness was slowly creeping over London...

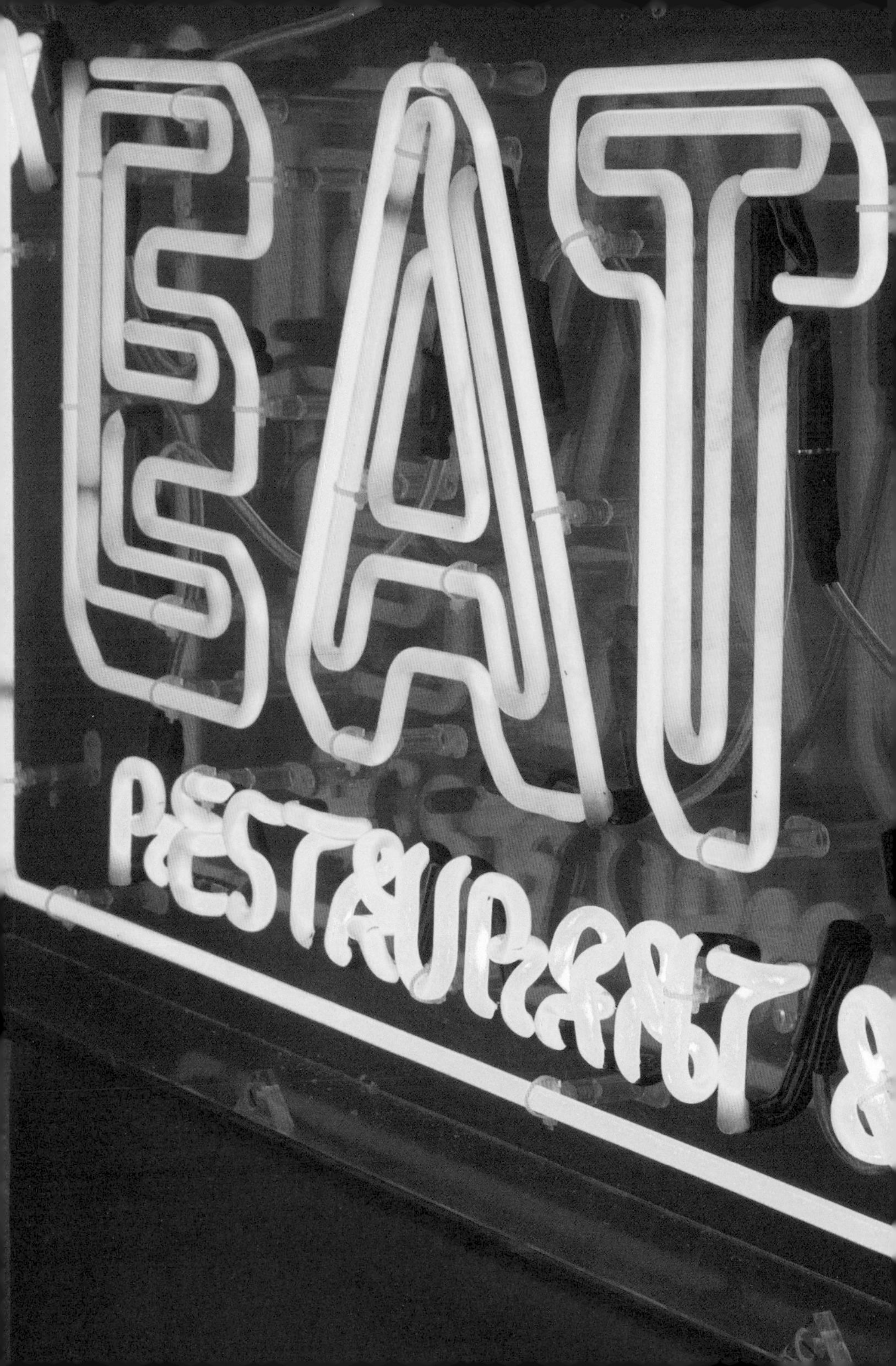
EAT
RESTAURANT

'Walk into most other convenience stores at 6pm and you'll find a mouldy steak bake on the hot plate, if you're lucky. We wanted to create restaurant-quality food in a shop.'
James Brundle, co-founder, Eat 17 (*Daily Telegraph*, June 2014)

It had always been meant for a burger, of course. That's how Eat 17 customers in Walthamstow were first introduced to Bacon Jam.

Chris used to top our Eat 17 hamburgers with a rasher of crispy bacon and caramelised onions. Walthamstow loved the burgers and everything seemed good with the world. But he wasn't satisfied. Was there a way to combine these two?

So he did some searching and he did some tasting. He took the bacon and the onions and he mixed in some strong coffee, a bit of maple syrup, some lemon, brown sugar, bourbon and thyme.

And suddenly there it was, the answer to his burger prayers – Bacon Jam.

When customers in the restaurant went mad for it and wanted some to take home, we put it in takeaway containers and sold it to them. When people in our shop wanted to buy it, we put it in a jar and stuck it on the shelves. Then when groceries, diners, delis, restaurants and supermarkets started calling and wanting to stock it in their own stores, our jam started popping up in all sorts of places.

Wedding bells & bacon: Eat 17 Bacon Jam jars do double-duty as tasty place settings at the wedding reception of former Walthamstow resisdents Dani and Tom.

Intersection of Bacon Street
and Brick Lane in east London.
Honorary home of British bacon.

I LOVE YOU LIKE GRILLED CHEESE AND BACON.

Let's just be clear. To many, Bacon Jam is simply a nice, easy way to get more bacon on everything. They haven't even considered that there might be some other ways they could put their pig-pink jar to good use. If you mention that they might be missing a trick, they cock their heads to one side and look at you in that way that your dog does sometimes when you open the drawer with the treats in it.

These uncomplicated bacon-lovers are perfectly happy to open up their jar of Bacon Jam and simply slap it on a burger, slather it on a sandwich or slop it on a nice piece of cheese see *The Instagram Walls of Fame* starting on page 18). You can see them sometimes, smiling to themselves, just before popping the seal on their latest Bacon Jam purchase and sitting down to consume the whole jar with nothing more than their favourite crackers and a nice wheel of brie. Bacon love, pure and simple. We can get behind that.

But there's much more to your Bacon Jam than this.

Eat 17's James Brindle and Chris O'Connor, lovers of bacon and makers of jam.

In an ode to our pink jar of bacon delight, Eat 17 suppliers, stockists, east London locals, meat-lovers and iconic London restaurants, shops and delis weigh in on how to get the most out of your jam.

Eat 17 has always been about great suppliers. From the very beginning, when we started out in Walthamstow Village, we wanted to update the idea of the convenience store. That was our mission. Why couldn't we offer different, quirky, unique products that you didn't often find in a corner shop? Why bother being the same as everyone else?

Since the launch of Bacon Jam, we've also been about great stockists. Our jam can be found in some of the most beautiful and best-loved shops and cafés in the UK, and you'll find Bacon Jam used on the cheese plates, burgers and sandwiches of a huge range of fantastic delis, diners and professional kitchens throughout the country.

So we've enlisted the help of over 30 Bacon Jam friends to show readers exactly how to get the most out of your jar of Bacon Jam. Some contributors show you exactly how they serve Bacon Jam to their customers (see Hank's Po' Boys and their Bacon Jam Smoky Mac 'n' Cheese on page 118), some incorporate Bacon Jam into what they do best (see Arancini Brothers' Bacon Jam Risotto Balls on page 84), and others get all carried away by an extreme bacon love of their own (Vicky's Donuts Maple Bacon Jam Donut bacon sarnie makeover on page 142). And keep an eye out for the Bacon Jam 💙 Beer icons where local brweries pair their beers with our bacon.

Albion
Roll out the bacon (and then get more bacon) on page 78

Arancini Brothers
Italian bacon is not pancetta, it's bacon (see page 84)

Balgove Larder
Scottish bacon love on page 58

Beaverton Brewery
Born in a BBQ joint under a bad sign, this beer is right at home with all things bacon

Born & Raised
Pizza really loves bacon jam on page 86

Cheese Posties
When in doubt, add bacon. Oh, and put a stamp on it, and go to page 92

Cooper & Wolf
Bacon goes to Sweden and the results are delicious on page 42

Courtyard Deli
If life gives you lemons, throw them away and get bacon (find out how on page 82)

Crate Brewery
In Hackney Wick, beer and pizza lovers come together (note: bacon is a good pizza topping)

Cutter & Squidge
S'more bacon, please (it's on page 138)

Deer Belly
You never realise how much you love bacon until it's gone (get more on page 112)

Duck & Waffle
Bacon is like meat candy (that's how it is 24-hours a day on page 44)

Eat 17
Creators of bacon in a jar and givers of the ability to put more bacon on everything

Fenton Poultry

Fenton Farm Eggs
Bacon and bacon jam and eggs belong together. So says page 108

The Five Points Brewing Company
Local, bacon-loving beer brewed in a Victorian railway arch in Hackney

The Fresh Past Company
Wrap everything in bacon and head over to p120

G Kelly
See page 70 for bunnies and bacon

Ginger's Kitchen
Shows you how to make things better with bacon on page 128

Hack & Veldt Delicatessen
A special occasion is any dish containing
bacon (psst: page 122)

Hank's Po' Boys
New Orleans wouldn't be the same without
bacon. Find out why on page 118

Holborn Dining Room
Classic pie gets a bacon-over on page 68

Muddy Boots
You either like bacon or you're wrong on
pages 48 and 60

Pearl & Groove
On page 140 there's chocolate *and* bacon

Pieminister
The fish and bacon pie on page 72 gets our
seal of approval

Pop's Kitchen
Caribbean spice meets bacon
on pages 50 and 74

The Saucy Fish Co.
Fish needs bacon too (page 62)

Señor Ceviche
On page 98, bacon makes all your problems
go away. That and a pisco sour

Soffle's Pitta Chips
Shows you the secret to their pitta chips
and then adds bacon, all on page 32

The Soho Sandwich Co.
Money can't buy happiness but it can buy
bacon, which is the same thing (page 94)

Sutton Hoo Chicken
Prize-winning chickens can't get enough
bacon (page 56)

Three Sods Brewery
Brewing from the Bethnal Green Working
Men's Club (bacon lovers since 1953)

Treflach Farm
The perfect scotch egg with bacon jam
is on page 110

Vicky's Donuts
Go quickly – there's bacon on a donut on
page 142!

Wildes Cheese
Cheese + bacon = wild happiness
(pages 130 and 134)

18 Instagram Wall of Fame: Bacon Jam in the Wild

It would be wrong to somehow suggest that our Eat 17 customers have one-track minds when it comes to their beloved Bacon Jam. As if the minute they're out the door, their jar of bacon bought and paid for, they spread it willy-nilly on the first comely grilled cheese or succulent burger that comes their way. We don't mean to imply that. Hence this Instagram Wall of Fame, where we prove that customers do indeed do loads of interesting, innovative, fun and tasty things with their jam, and are always kind enough to send us the photographic proof (check out the winner of our Instagram Bacon Jam recipe contest on page 22). This is pure, unadulterated Bacon Jam love in the wild, people. Like National Geographic for bacon. Enjoy. It's a beautiful thing.

'Let me tell you how totally delicious these homemade cheese scones were! Ridiculously delicious ... topped with a dollop of either bacon jam or chorizo jam. Soooooooo good!'

'Chilli bacon jam, avocado and poached eggs! Yum yum!'
'Oh yes please!!!'

'Sausage, pulled pork & bacon jam on a potato roll!'
'Looks amazing.'
'OMG bacon!'

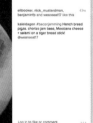

EAT 17

Nat Di Maggio's *Avocado, Coconut and Bacon Jam Ice Cream*

This dish was inspired by two things: my Sicilian grandmother's cooking and my recent three-month trip around South East Asia. My grandmother cooked an amazing pasta dish topped with salty anchovies and brown sugar which made every taste bud come alive. In Asia I fell in love with unusual flavour combinations too: palm sugar on fresh fish; deep fried sweet potatoes covered in chilli, salt and sugar. So it seemed only natural to add Bacon Jam to ice cream – it shouldn't work but it really does. Starts off sweet and creamy then turns slightly savoury.

Nat Di Maggio*, East London Makers Market

SERVES 4

1 very ripe avocado

2 ripe bananas

juice of 1 lime

1 x 400ml can full-fat coconut milk

1 tbsp clear honey

50g Bacon Jam

1 Remove the stone and skin from the avocado, and peel the bananas. Place in a blender and process until smooth. Alternatively, mash with a fork in a bowl.

2 Add the coconut milk, lime juice and honey, and blend/ mash again.

3 Stir in the Bacon Jam.

4 Pour into an ice cream machine and process until frozen, or pour into a container and place in the freezer, removing to stir with a fork every hour in order to break up ice crystals, until frozen.

5 As it will freeze to a solid block, remove from the freezer 30 mins before serving to soften slightly.

*Nat Di Maggio is a professional chef, community activist, art curator and most recently founded East London Makers Market, a monthly market and community of makers, bakers, artists and independent traders based in the iconic Leyton Town Hall. Nat has made Walthamstow his home for the last 23 years.

It's not just Bacon Jam. Eat 17 makes three other jams: Chilli Bacon Jam, Chorizo Jam and Onion Jam. Mix and match in any of the recipes if you feel the need. Experiment, taste and imagine what might make an interesting substitute. The Bacon and the Chilli Bacon jams are pretty interchangeable. The Bacon to Chorizo is a bit of a flavour leap but give it a try and see what works for you. The Onion is in a category all its own

Turn Up the Heat

Sometimes substitutions just make sense. Take heat. You just know when you're going to need more. Turn up the heat with a simple switch to Chilli Bacon Jam while still keeping it all in the bacon family. The Chilli Jam will do what it says on the label and add more heat but still give you a lovely bacon flavour.

Olé

Say bye bye bacon. Our Chorizo Jam uses – you guessed it – chorizo instead of bacon, plus some spices that make it oh so much more Spanish-y. Check out the jam substitution advice on the recipes that work great with this jam.

eat¹⁷

BACON JA

Born in our Eat 17 kitch

Walthamsto

Starters & Booze

Eat 17 *Bacon Jam & Mascarpone Crostini*

Soffle's *Olive Oil & Balsamic Pitta Chips with Bacon Jam*

Eat 17 *Bacon Jam Bourbon Mary*

Eat 17 *Bacon Jam Croquettes*

MAKES 1 BAGUETTE

1 demi-baguette

olive oil

mascarpone cheese

Bacon Jam

a handful of chives or
2 spring onions, finely
chopped

1 Preheat the oven to 200°C.

2 Slice the baguette into 3mm-thick rounds. Lay them flat on a baking sheet and drizzle with olive oil. Bake for 8–10 minutes until golden brown, then leave to cool.

3 Top with a spoonful of mascarpone and some Bacon Jam. Serve sprinkled with the chives or spring onions.

Pale

From Crate Brewery

(4.5% abv)

A fresh, aromatic single hopped ale bursting with tropical aromas.

32 Soffle's *Olive Oil & Balsamic Pitta Chips with Bacon Jam*

SERVES 4

4 pitta breads

olive oil

sea salt and freshly ground black pepper

balsamic reduction (store-bought or make your own, below)

105g Bacon Jam

'All good stores will sell a great balsamic reduction which might work more easily for you than making it yourself. If you are making it at home, however, perhaps make double the amount, just to be sure you have enough. Cooking temps and times may vary a little depending on your pitta so always keep an eye, turning the chips and possibly varying the time.'

Sophie Harvey, Soffle's Pitta Chips

Soffle's started out making their balsamic pitta chips in a converted shed in Stoke Newington. Now their pitta chips are found in shops like Eat 17 and pubs across London, where they are an amazing substitute for crisps alongside a beer.

1 Preheat the oven to 160°C.

2 Cut the pittas in half, and then split each half so you have the pitta completely open. Cut into triangles. Lay these pitta triangles out on baking trays without letting them overlap. Pour a good dose of olive oil over the chips (not so much that they'll be too oily but not so little that they'll roast dry). Season the chips with salt and pepper to taste.

3 Bake for about 15–20 minutes until crispy, shaking and turning the chips occasionally and making sure they don't burn.

4 Meanwhile, make the balsamic reduction. In a saucepan over a medium heat, mix 2 tbsp of brown sugar with one cup of balsamic vinegar and keep stirring until the sugar dissolves and the mixture comes to a boil. Turn the heat to low and simmer. Once the mixture is reduced by half (15–20 mins) and can coat the back of a spoon nicely, remove from the heat and leave to cool.

5 Increase the oven temperature to 200°C.

6 Squeeze the reduced balsamic vinegar in a generous zig-zag pattern across the chips. Place the chips back into the oven but watch them carefully so they don't burn. After a few minutes, as soon as you see the vinegar bubble, take them out of the oven. Leave them to cool.

7 Serve with lashings of Bacon Jam.

FOR THE MARY MIX

300ml Worcestershire sauce

100ml soft red wine such as French Grenache

80ml olive brine

20ml celery bitters

FOR THE BOURBON MARY

50ml bourbon

10ml lemon juice

1 tsp Bacon Jam

ice

100ml tomato juice

salt and freshly ground black pepper

celery stick and basil leaves, to garnish

'Bacon and bourbon live for each other. This Mary Mix recipe is for 500ml of mix, not just for an individual cocktail. Keep it sealed in the fridge and use it within two weeks.'
Martin Gray, Eat 17

1 Combine the Worcestershire sauce, wine, brine and bitters. This is your Mary mix.

2 Put the bourbon, lemon juice, Bacon Jam and 35ml of the Mary mix into a Boston glass and stir. Strain into another ice-filled glass, add the tomato juice and season with salt and pepper to taste.

3 Garnish with a celery stick and a few basil leaves before serving.

'This is the ultimate comfort food. Crispy, cheesy and, of course, bacony goodness. Once a batch is made, they freeze really well too, so they are very handy.'

Chris, Eat 17

**MAKES ABOUT
25 CROQUETTES**

75g butter

175g plain flour

450ml whole milk

100g Provolone cheese, grated

3 chives, chopped

105g Bacon Jam

3 eggs, beaten

200g panko breadcrumbs

rapeseed oil, for deep-frying

sea salt and freshly ground black pepper

1 Melt the butter in a heavy-based saucepan. When melted, add 75g of the flour and cook for 2 minutes, stirring, until flour is cooked out. Slowly add the milk, bit by bit, whisking as you add, then let the mix thicken over the heat for a few minutes, still stirring continuously. Beat in the eggs.

2 Fold in the cheese, chives and Bacon Jam and season with salt and pepper to taste. Pour the mixture into a large baking tray and allow to cool.

3 Take a tennis-ball size piece of the mixture and roll it out with your hands on a clean worktop until you have a long snake about the thickness of a thumb. Cut the whole thing into 3cm portions. Coat the pieces in a little flour and put in the freezer for 30 minutes.

4 Dip each piece at a time into the remaining flour, then into the beaten eggs, then the breadcrumbs.

5 Heat the deep-frying oil to 200°C, then add the croquettes in batches and fry for 2 minutes until they float to the surface but before the cheese starts to bubble out. Alternatively, fry them in a frying pan with a 1cm of hot oil. Lift out and drain on kitchen paper.

Bacon Jam & Beer

Mud Puddler Black IPA
From Three Sods Brewery

(4.9% abv)

Dark malts combined with fruitiness and spiciness.

THE FOLSOM

Meat

Eat 17 *Wild Boar & Bacon Jam Sausage Rolls*

Cooper & Wolf *Bacon Jam Swedish Meatballs*

Duck & Waffle *Bacon Jam Ox Cheeks*

Eat 17 *Chorizo Jam Pork Burger*

Muddy Boots *Bacon Jam Hamburger Patties*

Pop's Kitchen *Slow-Cooked Bacon Jam Chilli*

Eat 17 *Bacon Jam BBQ Sauce*

40 Eat 17 *Wild Boar & Bacon Jam Sausage Rolls*

MAKES 8

500g wild boar sausage meat or mince (or substitute pork)

1 tbsp dried sage

1 tsp English mustard

sea salt and freshly ground black pepper

500g puff pastry (shop-bought is fine)

a handful of flour, for dusting

105g Bacon Jam

2 eggs, beaten, to glaze

'We used to make our own sausage rolls when we first opened Eat 17 – venison and cranberry, pork, garlic and red onion marmalade, wild boar, sage and English mustard. Seeing as James and I could never do things by halves, we decided to make a few more to sell in the local farmers' market, then the local shops, delis and restaurants until soon we were supplying the whole of London. So we have loads of sausage roll experience and I'm sure these rolls below would have been top sellers.'

Chris, Eat 17

1 Preheat the oven to 200°C. Line a baking sheet with baking parchment.

2 Mix the wild boar meat with the sage and mustard, then season with salt and pepper. Scoop the mixture into a plastic piping bag, then snip off the end so you're left with a thumb-sized hole.

3 Roll out half the pastry on a lightly floured work surface to about 5mm thick. This should leave you with an A3-sized sheet.

4 Pipe the sausage meat evenly down the length of the pastry 2cm in from the long edge, avoiding any air bubbles. Pipe or spoon the Bacon Jam over the top of the sausage meat.

5 Brush the pastry on the narrow side of the sausage meat with the beaten egg, then fold the other side over the top and gently press the edges together to seal. Trim off the edge of the pastry using a sharp knife. You should have one long sausage roll in front of you.

6 Brush the top and sides with the egg wash, and crimp the recently closed edge of the pastry with a fork so it sticks firmly. Cut into four smaller sausage rolls. Repeat with the other half of the pastry.

7 Put the rolls on the prepared baking sheet and bake for 18 minutes until golden and cooked through.

42 Cooper & Wolf *Bacon Jam Swedish Meatballs*

'The Bacon Jam made the meatballs really moist and yummy but didn't overwhelm the original flavours.'

Sara Ratcliffe, Cooper & Wolf

SERVES 4

2 slices of bread

1 yellow onion, roughly chopped

100ml single cream

a handful of parsley

300g minced beef

450g minced pork

5 tbsp Bacon Jam

1 egg

sea salt and freshly ground black pepper

60g butter, plus extra for greasing

4–5 tbsp plain flour

450ml beef stock

200ml double cream

a splash of dark soy sauce

1 tbsp lingonberry jam or cranberry sauce, plus extra to serve

mashed potatoes and pickled cucumber, to serve

Just north of Eat 17 on Chatsworth Road near Millfields Park is Swedish café Cooper & Wolf*. They bake their own *kanelbullar* (traditional Swedish cinnamon buns), pickle their own herring and cure their own gravlax (salmon marinated in beetroot, lemon and dill) on the premises. This meatball recipe has been in the owner's family, minus the Bacon Jam, for generations.

1 Preheat the oven to 225°C. Lightly grease a baking sheet.

2 Mix together the bread, onion, single cream and parsley in a food processor or with a hand mixer, then tip into a bowl.

3 Add the beef, pork, Bacon Jam and egg to the mixture and season with salt and pepper. Carefully mix all the ingredients by hand until well blended.

4 Take pieces of the mixture and roll in the palms of your hands to the size of golf balls. You should get about 20–24. Place them on the prepared baking sheet with a few knobs of butter on top and bake for 20–25 minutes until cooked through and browned.

5 While they are cooking, make the beef stock. Melt the butter in a small saucepan over a low heat. Whisk in the flour to make a paste, then gradually whisk in the stock until smooth. Stir in the double cream, soy sauce and lingonberry jam, and season with salt and pepper. Simmer for about 5 minutes, stirring, to thicken the sauce.

6 Serve the meatballs covered in the sauce with a side of mashed potato, pickled cucumber and some more lingonberry jam.

East London Local E5

EAT 17

Duck & Waffle *Bacon Jam*
Ox Cheeks

Duck & Waffle* is a 24-hour restaurant like no other. With great food (including their namesake dish) from Group Executive Chef Dan Doherty, the restaurant boasts some of the best views over London from the 40th floor at 110 Bishopsgate – one of the City's tallest buildings. And then after your meal, you get to take the glass elevator all... the... way... down (one floor per second). Hold onto your duck and waffles.

SERVES 4

olive oil, for frying

2 ox cheeks, trimmed

1 onion, chopped into 2cm pieces

1 carrot, chopped into 2cm pieces

1 stick celery, chopped into 2cm pieces

2 garlic cloves, crushed

250ml red wine

400ml chicken stock

1 bay leaf

1 sprig of rosemary

1 sprig of thyme

2 tbsp Bacon Jam

FOR THE POLENTA

100g quick-cook polenta

about 400ml milk

20g butter

40g Parmesan cheese, grated

1 Preheat the oven to 160°C.

2 Heat a little olive oil in a frying pan, then seal the ox cheeks until brown on all sides. Transfer to an ovenproof casserole dish.

3 Add a little more oil to the pan, if necessary, add the onion, carrot, celery and garlic and sweat down until tender and taking a little colour.

4 Add the wine and boil to reduce it by 75 per cent, then pour the wine and vegetables over the ox cheeks. Add enough of the chicken stock to cover, then add the herbs. Cover and place in the oven for about 3 hours until the cheeks give way when pressed with a spoon. Allow to cool in the stock.

5 Gently lift out the ox cheeks and put on a tray. Strain the stock into a saucepan and put over a medium heat to simmer until it has reduced and starts to get a gravy-like consistency. Stir in the Bacon Jam and continue to reduce until you've got a thick, almost honey-like consistency, stirring frequently.

6 Return the ox cheeks to the pan and spoon over the sauce, glazing the cheeks all over. Cover and leave them to sit in the glaze over a very low heat while you prepare the rest of the dish.

7 To cook the polenta, follow the packet instructions, using milk instead of water, then add the butter and cheese and stir through.

8 To serve, spoon the polenta into bowls and pop a Bacon Jam-glazed cheek in each.

East London Local EC2N

Eat 17 *Chorizo Jam Pork Burger*

'This is a burger to end all burgers.'

Chris, Eat 17

MAKES 4

800g minced pork
(about 20% fat)

½ tsp paprika

½ tsp ground cumin

a pinch of chilli flakes

½ tsp sea salt

½ tsp freshly ground
black pepper

½ tsp soy sauce

½ tsp Worcestershire sauce

105g Chorizo Jam

4 brioche burger buns, split

4 tbsp aioli

a handful of baby spinach
leaves

100g Manchego cheese,
cut into 4 slices

1 Combine the minced pork with the paprika, cumin, chilli flakes, salt, pepper, soy sauce, Worcestershire sauce and 3 tablespoons of the Chorizo Jam*. Roll into 200g balls and chill, uncovered, for an hour or so. Shape into patties.

2 Heat a splash of oil in a frying pan over a medium heat and fry the burgers for 2–3 minutes each side until golden and cooked through.

3 Meanwhile, warm the brioche buns.

4 Spread the aioli on the bottom halves of the buns and top with the spinach. Slide the pork burger on top. Finish the burgers with a slathering of the remaining Chorizo Jam, a slice of Manchego cheese and the lid of the bun. Enjoy with a cold cerveza on the side.

Alternatively...

Incorporate the Bacon Jam directly into your burger patties for even more flavour. Eat 17 supplier, Muddy Boots, tells you how on page 49.

Best with our Chorizo Jam – even better than the Bacon!

Bacon Jam
& Beer

8 Ball (Rye IPA)
From Beaverton Brewery

(6.2% abv)

Originally made to accompany pulled pork and smoky ribs, this beer is a nice balance between hoppy and sweet. The ultimate beer for strong flavours.

48 Muddy Boots *Bacon Jam Hamburger Patties*

'I love using Bacon Jam in my kitchen for all sorts of recipes and as a cold accompaniment. I knew it would sell well in my shop, too, and it's a firm favourite with my customers.'

Miranda Ballard, Muddy Boots

**MAKES FOUR
200G BURGERS**

800g good-quality beef mince (15% fat)

8 tbsp Bacon Jam

8 spring onions, trimmed and finely chopped

4 large pinches of finely chopped fresh parsley

2 garlic cloves, finely chopped (optional)

sea salt and freshly ground black pepper

a little oil, for frying

From their family farm in Worcestershire and their Modern Meat Shop in Crouch End, Muddy Boots* supplies Eat 17 with ready-to-use beef burgers in flavours like lamb and mint, caramelised onion and mozzarella, and beetroot and Bramley apple.

1 Mix all the ingredients together in a bowl using your hands so the flavours get completely mixed through the minced beef.

2 Squeeze the mixture into 4 balls and flatten evenly into burgers.

3 Heat a little oil in a heavy-based frying pan and fry the burgers until cooked through and browned on both sides.

Eat 17 Supplier, Stockist & London Local N8

'Bacon Jam gives a simple meal a little extra edge.'

Marie Mitchell, Pop's Kitchen

SERVES 4

450g stewing beef, diced

1 tbsp cornflour

2 tsp sea salt

2 tbsp olive oil

1 large onion, finely chopped

2 garlic cloves, crushed

20g root ginger, grated

2 tsp ground cumin

1 tsp ground coriander

400g tin of chopped tomatoes

400g tin of kidney beans

120ml red wine

500ml beef stock

1 scotch bonnet pepper, deseeded and finely chopped

3 tbsp Bacon Jam

2 tbsp tomato purée

2 tsp Worcestershire sauce

TO SERVE

cooked rice

1 lime, cut into wedges

½ bunch of coriander, leaves only

1 avocado

A few miles from Eat 17 in Hackney, Marie Mitchell runs a Caribbean supper club with the help of her family (her dad Earl being the 'Pop' in Pop's Kitchen*), cooking traditional Caribbean favourites like ackee and salt fish tartlets, Jamaican patties and freshy baked hard dough with a British touch.

1 Preheat the oven to 160°C.

2 Sprinkle the beef with the cornflour and sea salt and mix well. Heat the oil in a large, flameproof casserole dish and cook the beef pieces for a few minutes each side over a high heat until browned all over. Remove from the pan and set aside.

3 In the same dish, cook the onion over a medium heat until softened. Stir in the garlic, ginger, cumin and ground coriander and continue stirring for 1 minute. Add the tomatoes. Drain the kidney beans, reserving the liquid, and put the beans to one side. Add the reserved liquid to the pan with another ½ can of water. Stir the meat back in.

4 Add the wine, beef stock, scotch bonnet, Bacon Jam, tomato purée and Worcestershire sauce. Cook covered for 3–4 hours or until the meat is incredibly tender. When cooked, add the kidney beans, re-cover and leave to sit for 10 minutes.

5 Serve on a bed of rice with lime wedges, chopped coriander leaves and sliced avocado.

*East London Local E8

'Liquid smoke gives the finished sauce a nice lift. A bit of a shortcut but it does the job. You'll find it in most supermarkets.'

Chris, Eat 17

MAKES ABOUT 250G

1 brown onion, thinly sliced

3 garlic cloves, minced

4 tbsp olive oil

1 tsp paprika

1 tsp cayenne pepper

1 tsp ground cumin

½ tsp sea salt

½ tsp white pepper

200ml passata

100g light soft brown sugar

105g Bacon Jam

generous 2 tbsp Worcestershire sauce

2 tbsp Dijon mustard

generous 2 tbsp balsamic vinegar

1 tbsp liquid smoke essence

4 tsp soy sauce

1 Fry the onion and garlic in the oil until just beginning to soften. Add the paprika, cayenne, cumin, salt and pepper and continue to cook until the onions are softened. Stir in the passata, sugar, Bacon Jam, Worcestershire sauce and mustard and cook for 5 minutes.

2 Add the vinegar, essence and soy sauce and simmer until the liquid has reduced by one-third and the mixture is somewhat sticky.

3 Blend the reduced mix with a hand blender directly in the pan or transfer to a food processor or blender and purée until smooth. Leave to cool.

4 Store in the fridge to use at your next barbecue – it's fantastic on ribs. Marinate in the sauce and baste while cooking, or just serve on the side.

Bacon Jam & Beer

London Smoke
From The Five Points Brewing Company

(7.8% abv)

A lightly-smoked imperial porter brewed with smoked barley and wheat malt.

Opposite: an Eat 17 Walthamstow sous chef guards his Bacon Jam BBQ sauce-covered rack of ribs

eat " BACON JAM

Jean Jullie

Poultry & Seafood

Sutton Hoo *Bacon Jam Chicken & Rice*

Balgove Larder *Bacon Jam
Pigeon Breasts & Lentils*

Muddy Boots *Bacon Jam-Stuffed Chicken
Thighs*

The Saucy Fish Co. *Bacon Jam Salmon*

Eat 17 *Scallops with Bacon Jam*

'Bacon Jam should go in every chicken sandwich made the day after a roast.'

Will Waterer, Sutton Hoo Chicken

SERVES 4

8 chicken thighs

2–3 tbsp olive oil

3 garlic cloves, crushed

50g pine nuts

150ml white wine

850ml chicken stock

3 heaped tbsp Bacon Jam

1 tsp sea salt

340g long-grain rice

green vegetables, to serve

On the Suffolk coast about 85 miles from Eat 17, much-loved family farm Sutton Hoo Chicken has been producing slow grown, free-range, drug-free, super-tasty chickens for more than 20 years. We can't get enough of their chicken burgers and vacuum-packed, marinated spatchcocks.

1 Preheat the oven to 190°C.

2 In a large frying or griddle pan, brown the chicken thighs on all sides in the oil. Remove from the pan and set aside.

3 In the same pan, place the crushed garlic with the pine nuts and toss until the nuts are toasted light brown. Add the white wine, chicken stock, Bacon Jam and salt and bring to the boil, mixing well to scrape up any bits that might have stuck to the pan.

4 Stir in the rice and blend well, then pour it all into a large ovenproof serving dish. Place the reserved chicken pieces evenly on top of the rice mixture and cover with foil.

5 Cook in the oven for 60–70 minutes. By this time, the rice should have absorbed all the stock and the chicken will be succulent and browned. Serve with any green vegetable.

'Bacon jam is one of those "inquisitive ingredients" – the type that really gets people guessing about how you've made something so delicious. We've been stocking Bacon Jam since it first came to market and Scotland officially loves it!'

Will Docker, Balgove Larder

Balgove Larder is based just outside St Andrews in Fife and focuses on showcasing fantastic Scottish and British foods. What they don't rear, grow or breed there on their farm, they source from trusted producers – and they stock Eat 17 Bacon Jam.

SERVES 4

extra virgin olive oil

1 large onion, diced

2 celery sticks, diced

1 carrot, diced

500g Puy lentils

1.5 litres chicken stock

8 wood pigeon breasts (or guinea fowl, partridge or pheasant)

1 bunch of flat-leaf parsley, roughly chopped

6 sprigs of thyme, leaves picked

sea salt and freshly ground black pepper

105g Bacon Jam

green salad, to serve

1 Place a heavy-based pan over a medium-high heat. Add a good glug of olive oil, followed by the diced onion and cook for 4 minutes, stirring. Add the celery and carrot. Continue stirring for a further 4 minutes. Season with a small amount of salt and pepper.

2 Add the lentils and stir for 30 seconds. Pour in 1 litre of the chicken stock and bring up to a light simmer for 20 minutes. Add 400ml of the remaining chicken stock as required – the lentils should finish up absorbing most of the liquid.

3 Place another frying pan over a high heat. Brush the pigeon breasts with olive oil and season with salt and pepper. Cook the breasts for 2 minutes on each side, then remove from the heat. Cover with foil.

4 Add most of the parsley and thyme to the lentils with a glug of olive oil. Stir and season with salt and pepper to taste.

5 Place the pigeon on a chopping board and slice the meat on the diagonal. Pour the remaining 100ml of chicken stock into the frying pan and bring to the boil, stirring to mix in anything stuck to the bottom of the pan. Stir in the Bacon Jam until mixed through the stock.

6 To serve, scoop the lentils and meat into the centre of each plate. Spoon over the Bacon Jam jus. Garnish with the remaining herbs and serve with a green salad.

SERVES 2

8 tsp cream cheese

8 tsp Bacon Jam

4 tsp finely chopped fresh chives, plus extra for sprinkling

4 boneless, skin-on chicken thighs

sea salt and freshly ground black pepper

4–8 tbsp olive oil

1 garlic clove, finely chopped

8 spring onions, trimmed and left whole

1 Preheat the oven to 180°C.

2 Mix the cream cheese, Bacon Jam and chives in a bowl. Lay each thigh skin-side down on a chopping board and spread the mixture over the boneless inside. Wrap the skin around the inside filling and pin together with two cocktail sticks, making sure the skin is pulled as tightly as possible.

3 Lay the thighs skin-side down on a baking tray and put in the oven with another tray underneath to catch any spills. Cook for 10 minutes, and then turn the thighs over, sprinkling with a pinch of salt and pepper and a drizzle a little olive oil on each. Cook for a further 10 minutes until cooked through and browned on the top.

4 Meanwhile, heat the remaining olive oil in a frying pan and fry the chopped garlic for 3–4 minutes until browned. Add the spring onions and fry for 4–5 minutes until they start to soften and brown.

5 When the chicken is ready, cross the spring onions on a small plate and lay the chicken thighs on top. Use the creamy oils from the roasting dish to pour over the top and sprinkle with some more fresh chives.

Muddy Boots – *Eat 17 Supplier & London Local N8*

'Bacon Jam on fish? We're converts! The intense smoky flavour of the jam really compliments the delicate taste of the salmon.'

Anne Laudage, Brand Manager at The Saucy Fish Co.

SERVES 4

3 slices white sandwich bread

50g fresh parsley

2 tbsp olive oil

4 skinless salmon fillets

105g Bacon Jam

225g cherry tomatoes

From Grimsby, The Saucy Fish Co. sends its fish and sauce pairings all over the UK, making cooking fish that much more convenient. Their mission is to get more fish on more plates.

1 Preheat the oven to 200°C and line a baking sheet with baking parchment.

2 Put the bread, parsley and a tablespoon of the oil in a food processor and mix until small crumbs begin to form.

3 Place the salmon fillets on the prepared baking sheet. Spread an extra-generous amount of Bacon Jam on the top of each fillet. Sprinkle the breadcrumbs on top. Put the cherry tomatoes in a separate roasting tray. Bake both in the oven for 12–15 minutes until the fish is tender and the breadcrumbs are lightly browned, and the cherry tomatoes are soft.

4 Serve the fillets on a bed of roasted cherry tomatoes.

1 small celeriac, peeled and cut into thumb-sized chunks

50g butter

200ml milk

sea salt and freshly ground black pepper

olive oil

8 large scallops

½ jar Bacon Jam

1 recipe quantity Bacon Jam Crumbs (see page 127)

1 Put the celeriac in a heavy-based pan with half the butter and cook over a medium heat for a few minutes, without allowing it to brown. Season with a little salt.

2 Add the milk, stir and bring to the boil, then cover and simmer for 20 minutes until celeriac is soft, stirring occasionally. Leave to cool slightly, then purée to a fine consistency. Season with salt and pepper to taste. Set aside but keep warm.

3 Heat the remaining butter and a little oil in a heavy-based pan and cook the scallops for about 2 minutes on each side until golden.

4 Serve the scallops and celeriac on a bed of Bacon Jam. Scatter with Toasted Bacon Jam Crumbs (page 127) for a bit of a crunch.

Gamma Ray
From Beaverton Brewery

(5.4% abv)

An American Pale with juicy, exotic tones and a fresh, full-on hoppy body.

Pies

Holborn Dining Room *Bacon Jam Steak & Kidney Pudding*

G. Kelly *Rabbit, Bacon & Bacon Jam Pie*

Pieminister *Smoked Haddock, Cider & Bacon Jam Pie*

Pop's Kitchen *Bacon Jam Cottage Pie*

SERVES 4

FOR THE PASTRY

100g butter, frozen then grated, plus extra for greasing

140g cold, shredded beef suet

375g cold self-raising flour, plus extra for dusting

1½ tsp sea salt

130ml ice-cold water

'The pudding gets an element of wonderful sweetness from the Bacon Jam.'

Calum Franklin, Holborn Dining Room

Holborn Dining Room* has a lovely little deli just off High Holborn where you can find our Bacon Jam among the other jars and jams and delicacies from all over the world.

1 Preheat the oven to 160°C and butter the inside of a 2-litre pudding basin.

2 Put the grated butter, suet, self-raising flour and salt in a bowl and mix together well with a butter knife. Add the cold water a little at a time, still mixing with the butter knife. Gently and briefly knead by hand to bring the mixture together into a dough (you should still be able to see flecks of butter and suet through the mix). If the dough gets overworked, the mix will become dry, tough and expand too much when steamed. Wrap the dough tightly in clingfilm and let it rest in the fridge for at least an hour.

3 Put the diced beef in a large bowl with the plain flour and toss to coat well, then transfer the meat to a dish, dusting off the excess, and retain the remaining flour for later.

4 Heat a little oil in a large frying pan and fry the meat in small batches until well browned, then remove from the pan using a slotted spoon and set aside. Get the pan very hot again and fry the kidney chunks until well browned, then set aside. Add the onions, garlic, thyme, bay leaf and cayenne to the pan with 160g of the butter and cook until the onion is soft.

5 Add the reserved flour and cook for 5 minutes, stirring. Add the wine and boil until reduced by half. Add the

FOR THE FILLING

2kg braising chuck beef, diced into 5cm pieces

200g plain flour

1 ox kidney (approx. 500g), diced into 5cm chunks, white fat or membrane removed

a little oil, for frying

3 large Spanish onions, finely chopped

2 garlic cloves, finely chopped

2 tsp chopped thyme

1 bay leaf

½ tsp cayenne

175g unsalted butter

100ml white wine

3 litres hot beef stock

sea salt and freshly ground black pepper

75g Bacon Jam

buttered, peppered cabbage and sprouting broccoli, to serve

*Bacon Jam Stockist & London Local WC1V

beef stock, bring to boil and season well. Put all the meat into the sauce and stir in the Bacon Jam. Transfer to an ovenproof dish and cover with foil. Cook in the oven for 1–1½ hours until the meat is tender.

6 Remove the meats from the dish with a slotted spoon and set aside. Return the sauce to the pan and boil over a medium heat until reduced and thickened enough to hold the meat in the pudding well. Combine the meat and sauce again and chill in a bowl.

7 Roll out the suet pastry on a lightly floured surface to a circle 1cm thick. Place the pudding basin top-down on the pastry as a guide and cut out a circle 7.5cm wider than the circumference of the basin. Repeat once more, this time just cutting exactly around the shape of the basin to form the lid. Take the first, larger disc and slide it down into the pudding bowl, making sure there are no air bubbles at the bottom and the pastry just slightly overlaps at the top of the basin. Fill the pastry right up with the meat and sauce mixture. Cover it all with the smaller disc, which is your lid. Wet the pastry with a little cold water to fold over the edges of the overlapping pastry, forming a seal and finishing the pudding.

8 Wrap the whole thing tightly with clingfilm so it's airtight and place in a baking tray, then fill the tray with boiling water to come halfway up the basin (a bain marie). Bake in the oven for 4 hours, topping up the boiling water around the basin halfway through.

9 To serve, remove the clingfilm from the basin and carefully turn out the pudding onto a large plate. Sprinkle with sea salt. Serve with buttered, peppered cabbage and sprouting broccoli.

G. Kelly *Rabbit, Bacon & Bacon Jam Pie*

MAKES A 25CM PIE

100g unsmoked streaky bacon, cut into lardons or rough dice

2 rabbits, jointed

250ml dry cider

2 carrots, quartered

3 celery sticks, quartered

1 large onion, quartered

250g chestnut mushrooms, quartered

a little oil, for frying and greasing

1 heaped tbsp butter

1 heaped tbsp plain flour, plus extra for dusting

2 tbsp Bacon Jam

½ tsp white pepper

500g rough puff pastry

1 egg, beaten

'As World War 2 rationing began, my grandfather negotiated a meat quota from the Ministry of Food which allowed us to stay open for business, even after our shop front was blown away during the Blitz. A wartime staple, rabbit was often part of our ration.'

Neil Vening of G. Kelly, Roman Road Market

Originally opened in 1937, this classic pie & mash shop is located in Roman Road in the heart of East London.*

1 Preheat the oven to 150°C.

2 Gently fry the bacon in a large frying pan until lightly browned, then transfer to a large ovenproof dish using a slotted spoon, leaving the fat behind. Brown the rabbit joints in the bacon fat, a few pieces at a time, moving them to the ovenproof dish once they're golden brown all over.

3 Pour the cider into the pan and bring to the boil, stirring to mix in any bits on the bottom of the pan, then pour into the ovenproof dish, adding the carrots, celery and onion. Top up the liquid in the dish with water until the rabbit is almost covered, then stir. Cook in the oven for 1¼ hours until the meat easily pulls away from the bone. If it does not, bake for an additional 15 minutes.

4 Lift the rabbit meat into a bowl using a slotted spoon and leave to cool. Lift out and discard the vegetables. Once cool enough to touch, remove the bones and break the meat into generous pieces. Return the sauce to a saucepan and boil to reduce the remaining stock to about 750ml.

5 While the stock is reducing, fry the mushrooms in the oil until the moisture is driven off and they start to brown. Add to the rabbit.

6 Preheat the oven to 200°C and grease a 25cm pie dish.

7 Melt the butter in the frying pan and whisk in the flour to form a roux. Gradually add the stock, whisking as you go, followed by the Bacon Jam and white pepper. Heat until the gravy stops thickening. Add the gravy to the rabbit and stir until evenly distributed.

8 Set aside one-third of the pastry for the pie lid. Roll out the remaining pastry on a lightly floured surface and use it to line the pie dish, gently pressing down the pastry so it conforms to the shape of the dish. Fill the lined dish to the top with the rabbit filling (if you have any excess, save it to make a ragu later). Now roll out the remaining pastry to the same thickness but slightly larger than the pie dish. Brush the exposed bottom pastry rim with the beaten egg before laying the top pastry over the filling so that both sheets meet around the entire circumference. Press around the rim using a fork to seal the pie and leave an attractive finish. Use a large knife to cut a cross in the centre of the pie to allow steam to escape. Brush the pie top with the remaining beaten egg.

9 Bake in the oven for 35 minutes or until golden brown. Leave to rest for 15 minutes before serving.

East London Local E3

'This is a fish pie that is probably bad for the heart but damned good for the sole.'

Tristan Hogg, Pieminister

Pieminister* is an award-winning family pie business based in Bristol that uses free range British meat and makes all its pies in-house. Bestsellers at Eat 17 include the Free Ranger (free-range British chicken, ham hock with leek and West Country Cheddar), the Moo (British beef steak, cracked black pepper and real ale) and the Vegetarian Society approved Heidi pie (Somerset goats' cheese, sweet potato, spinach and red onion).

SERVES 4

750g new potatoes, scrubbed

40g butter

3 shallots, sliced

2 fat leeks, sliced

3 plump garlic cloves, finely chopped

1 heaped tbsp plain flour

400ml good-quality medium cider

1 tbsp wholegrain mustard

150ml double cream

sea salt and freshly ground black pepper

500g undyed smoked haddock, skinned and cut into large chunks

60g Bacon Jam

a few sprigs of thyme or rosemary, leaves picked and chopped

olive oil, for drizzling

80g mature Cheddar cheese, grated

steamed green beans tossed in butter or mixed salad and a glass of cider, to serve

1 Preheat the oven to 180°C.

2 Cook the potatoes in boiling salted water until tender, then drain and leave until cool enough to handle. Cut into fairly thick slices and set aside.

3 Melt the butter in a large, ovenproof frying pan (if you don't have one, use any frying pan and transfer the entire mixture to a shallow ovenproof dish before putting it in the oven). Add the shallots, leeks and garlic and cook gently until soft.

4 Stir in the flour and cook for a minute, stirring, then gradually pour in the cider, stirring constantly. Bring to a simmer and cook gently for about 5 minutes. Stir in the mustard and cream and season to taste with salt and pepper. Remove from the heat and add the fish, stirring gently to coat it in the sauce. Dot spoonfuls of Bacon Jam across the top of the mix.

5 Put the sliced potatoes in a bowl, add the thyme or rosemary and drizzle with olive oil. Toss until the potatoes are evenly coated in the oil, then season with salt and pepper. Lay the potatoes over the fish mixture and scatter the cheese on top. Place in the oven and bake for about 30 minutes, until the topping is nicely browned.

6 Serve with lightly steamed green beans tossed in butter or a dressed green salad and a large glass of cider.

*Eat 17 Supplier

1 Preheat the oven to 220°C.

2 Heat olive oil in a large saucepan over a medium heat. Add the mince and brown, salting it with a few pinches of sea salt. Once browned, remove from the pan and set aside.

3 Add the onion, shallots, carrots and celery to the pan with a little more oil, if needed to avoid sticking. Cook for about 15 minutes, or until softened. Add the garlic and tomato purée and cook for a few minutes, stirring.

4 Return the beef to the pan, sprinkle with the flour and stir well. Pour the wine over the top and simmer, stirring, to reduce it slightly, then stir in the stock, Bacon Jam and Worcestershire sauce. Bring to a simmer, then add the scotch bonnet, thyme and bay leaves. Cook, uncovered, for about 45 minutes until rich and thick. Allow to cool a little so the potatoes don't sink when you assemble the dish.

5 Meanwhile, peel and roughly chop the potatoes. Put in a large saucepan, cover them in salted cold water, bring to the boil, then simmer until tender. Drain and steam-dry for a minute or two. Mash well with the milk and butter, then stir in the spring onions and season to taste with salt and pepper.

6 Spoon the slightly cooled meat mixture into an ovenproof dish and cover with the mash. Sprinkle the Parmesan evenly over the mash with a little freshly ground black pepper. Cook for 25 minutes, or until the dish is hot throughout and the Parmesan is golden. For a lovely, crispy topping, flash the pie quickly under the grill for a minute or two before serving.

SERVES 4

1 tbsp olive oil

500g good quality, lean beef mince

1 onion, finely chopped

2 shallots, finely chopped

2 carrots, peeled, quartered and cut into chunks

2 celery sticks, roughly chopped and leaves removed

2 garlic cloves, crushed

2 tbsp tomato purée

1 tbsp plain flour

150ml red wine

500ml beef stock

2 tbsp Bacon Jam

2 tbsp Worcestershire sauce

1 scotch bonnet hot pepper, whole

6–7 sprigs of thyme

3 bay leaves

800g good mashing potatoes

70ml milk

90g butter

2 spring onions, finely chopped

sea salt and freshly ground black pepper

50g Parmesan cheese, grated

Pop's Kitchen – *East London Local E8*

Cheese

Albion *Bacon Jam Stilton Rolls*

Eat 17 *Deep-Fried Manchego with Chorizo Jam*

Courtyard Deli *Stout Welsh Bacon Jam Rarebit*

Arancini Brothers *Bacon Jam Risotto Balls*

Born & Raised *Bacon Jam and Broccoli Pizza*

'Bacon Jam's also great as a dip for a bread stick and a glass of wine.

Aurelien Beguyot, Albion

MAKES 8 ROLLS

600g white bread flour, plus extra for dusting

370ml water

12g sea salt

12g fresh yeast

210g Bacon Jam

130g Stilton cheese (we used Colston Bassett), crumbled

Albion* is a bakery and café in the heart of busy Shoreditch with a hotel attached (or is that a hotel with a bakery and a café attached?). Their little shop stocks loads of different British food and drink brands among the fresh bread, pastries and salads for takeaway.

1 Line a baking sheet with baking parchment.

2 Using a stand mixer, or by hand, knead the flour, water, salt and yeast together for around 10 minutes, just like making a normal bread dough. Once kneaded, store the dough in a floured, covered bowl, making sure that the cover never touches the dough. Let it prove for an hour until it doubles in size.

3 Once the dough is ready, roll it out on a lightly floured surface into a 40cm x 60cm 4mm-thick rectangle. With a palette knife, spread the Bacon Jam all over the dough, as evenly as possible. Scatter pieces of Stilton on top of the jam.

4 From the longest edge, roll the dough as tightly as possible, as if making a Swiss roll. Cut the roll into 8 small rolls and let them rest on the prepared baking sheet for about 1 hour until they have almost doubled in size.

5 Preheat the oven to 220°C after the rolls have been proving for 45 minutes.

6 Bake for about 15 minutes, or until the rolls are a light golden colour.

Bacon Jam Stockist & East London Local E2

3 tbsp plain flour

1 egg, beaten

6 tbsp panko crumbs

200g Manchego cheese, cut into 8 fingers

oil, for frying

105g Chorizo Jam, to serve

1 Put the flour, the egg and panko crumbs in 3 separate shallow dishes. Roll the cheese fingers in the flour, dip in the egg, then coat with the panko crumbs.

2 Heat 1cm of oil in a heavy-based frying pan or deep-frying oil to 200°C. Gently lower in the cheese fingers and fry for 2 minutes until crisp and golden. Drain on kitchen paper.

3 Serve with Chorizo Jam*.

Best with our Chorizo Jam – even better than the Bacon!

Bacon Jam & Beer

Five Points Pale
From The Five Points Brewing Company

(4.4% abv)

A pale ale with zippy, clean flavours. An amazing friend to fried foods and cheese.

82 Courtyard Deli *Stout Welsh Bacon Jam Rarebit*

SERVES 4

440ml can of dark stout (we use Guinness)

50g butter

50g plain flour

500ml milk

100g mature Cheddar cheese, grated

1 tbsp English mustard

1 tbsp Worcestershire sauce

1 egg yolk

sea salt and freshly ground black pepper

4 thick slices of sourdough bread

105g Bacon Jam

mixed salad, to serve (optional)

'I've spread the Bacon Jam underneath the cheese prior to grilling, which gives it a really great sweet onion/bacon note that stands up well against the strong, stout rarebit. Simple but really tasty and comforting.'

Chris Biggers, Courtyard Deli

Ex-army, Cordon Bleu-trained chef, Chris and former caterer, Sarah, are the husband and wife team who run The Courtyard Deli in Falmouth, Cornwall. You'll find our Bacon Jam both in their shop and on their menu, featured in classic, tasty rarebits like this one.

1 Pour the stout into a saucepan over a high heat and boil for about 10 minutes to reduce to a syrup. If you take it too far, just add a splash of water to bring it back to the correct consistency. Set aside and leave to cool.

2 Melt the butter in a saucepan over a medium heat. Add the flour and cook, stirring, until the mixture has a sand-like texture. Turn the heat down low and add one-third of the milk. Gently whisk this into the butter/flour mixture until you have a smooth paste. Add the next third of milk and whisk in again, ensuring there are no lumps. Finally add the remaining milk. Turn the heat up to medium and continue stirring until the sauce starts to bubble. Cook for a further 5 minutes, stirring all the time.

3 Remove from the heat and add the Cheddar, mustard, Worcestershire sauce, egg yolk and stout syrup. The egg yolk ensures that the mixture will colour nicely under the grill. Taste and season with salt and pepper. You may need to add a little more mustard or Worcestershire sauce if you like it extra punchy. You can store this mixture in a sealed container for up to a week in the fridge.

4 When ready to make the sandwich, take your sourdough and chargrill both sides on a hot griddle pan. If you don't have a griddle pan, just pop the slices under a grill until both sides are golden brown.

5 Make sure your grill is screaming hot. Spread a generous amount of Bacon Jam on one side of each slice and top that with a thick layer of the stout rarebit paste. Grill until the mixture is bubbling and blistering on top. The blackened, caramelised patches are the best bits!

6 Serve with a green side salad (if feeling healthy) or (if not) just eat two slices instead of one.

'It's easy to make our little risotto ball but not that easy. Enjoy getting it not quite right, then refine and change. That's how we ended up with this recipe in the first place.'

Dave Arkin, Arancini Brothers*

Big Dave and Little Dave have been in the restaurant business since they were 16. Starting out as a tiny market stall on the Sunday morning Brick Lane market, they progressed to festivals and other markets before opening their own shop, where they sell their famous risotto balls, home-baked sweets and top-notch coffee.

MAKES 20 RISOTTO BALLS

1 litre vegetable stock

2 large brown onions, finely diced

1 garlic bulb, all cloves finely diced

50g salted butter

2 tbsp extra virgin olive oil

250g Arborio rice

2 tbsp chopped fresh thyme

grated zest and juice of 1 lemon

grated zest and juice of 1 orange

150g mozzarella cheese, shredded

100g Cheddar cheese, grated

100g Parmesan cheese, grated

3 tbsp finely chopped chives

6 tbsp finely chopped parsley

sea salt and freshly ground black pepper

100g rice flour

105g Bacon Jam

vegetable oil, for frying

1 Bring the vegetable stock to the boil in a small saucepan. Meanwhile, in a large saucepan, fry the onions and garlic in the butter and a dash of oil until soft. Just before they start to colour, add the rice and thyme and continue to fry for 1 minute, stirring to make sure the mixture does not stick.

2 Add about 250ml of stock to the rice mixture every 3 minutes, never ceasing to stir. The idea is to let all the stock absorb before adding more. Try and soak up all the remaining stock over 15 minutes or so. When the rice has absorbed all the liquid and is nice and firm with no hard core in the middle of the grain, remove the pan from the heat and spread the mixture over a large oven tray to cool it quickly for 25 minutes.

3 Once the rice is cool to touch, scoop it back into the large pan and mix in the cheese, herbs and fruit zest and juice. Add salt and pepper to taste.

4 Put the rice flour into a clean, shallow bowl.

5 With slightly wet hands, make golf ball-sized balls out of the rice and cheese mixture, pressing your thumb into the middle of each to fill it with about a teaspoon of Bacon Jam. Cover the filled hole and roll the balls back into golf-ball shapes. Dust in rice flour and place on the baking tray. Cover with clingfilm and chill for 1 hour.

6 To cook, shallow-fry in 1.5cm of hot vegetable oil for about 5 minutes, turning when light brown. You can also deep-fry them, if you want to.

East London Local E8

EAT 17

DOUGH

1kg of '00' high gluten flour

6g dried yeast

600ml cold water

20g salt

TO TOP EACH PIZZA

50g mozzarella

2 tender stems of broccoli

small handful of curly kale

4 tsp Bacon Jam

a few slices of red onion

3 sage leaves

drizzle of olive oil

'The jam was a great way to add a sweet and tangy flavour to the pizza, and complements the broccoli and kale beautifully.'
Tom Dewey, Born & Raised

Growing up in Lincolnshire, Tom loved two things: the wood-fired pizzas he ate on holidays in the south of France, and his family's Land Rover. So it made total sense when he converted a Defender 110 into a mobile oven to create locally-sourced British pizza. Popular combinations include goats cheese with caramalised onions and watercress on a beetroot-infused sourdough, and beef brisket and horseradish cream.

1 Pour the flour into a large bowl. Dissolve the yeast in the water and pour into the bowl of flour. Using your fingertips, start to bring together the flour and water mixture. Once the water begins to mix with the flour, sprinkle the salt into the bowl and fully mix until it forms a dough. Knead for about 10 minutes then allow to relax (uncovered) in a bowl for 5 minutes, before kneading again for 5 minutes.

2 Now divide the dough into nine 190 gram balls, that you can roll into shape on the kitchen worktop. Then place the balls in a floured sealed container, or baking tray covered with cling film – don't use a wet tea towel; make sure they are sealed. Leave a good inch of space around each dough ball, to allow it to rise. Leave in the fridge overnight (or for two nights maximum). Once they have risen, you can wrap any dough balls in cling film and refrigerate for up to two days.

3 Prepare the toppings so you are ready to go when cooking the pizza (it all happens quite quickly like a stir fry, so have everything ready). Cut the mozzarella into small cubes; cook the broccoli for 2 minutes in boiling salted water, then refresh in a bowl of iced water; then do the same with the kale.

4 Heat a dry frying pan on the stove or turn the grill onto high, depending on whether you're going to cook this pizza in a frying pan or a pizza oven. Take one of the dough balls carefully out of the container with a spatula. On a floured surface, use your fingertips to start pushing the dough ball out from the centre, ensuring that you keep a nice, even, round shape. As you push the dough outwards, leave a centimetre around the edge that you don't touch (to allow the crust to rise).

5 Turn the ball over and repeat, with plenty of flour underneath the dough. Once the dough has doubled in size you can carefully stretch it outwards until the pizza it around 10 inches in diameter – roughly the same size as your pan.

6 Very carefully lift the dough up and place it in the frying pan – it will start to cook and rise instantly. Sprinkle mozzarella onto the pizza, then add the broccoli, kale, onion and sage leaves, spreading them out evenly over the base. Spoon a little Bacon Jam over the pizza and finish with a drizzle of olive oil. As soon as you have topped the pizza, place it straight under the grill in the pan and leave for 3 to 4 minutes or until the dough starts to brown. This can happen very quickly.

7 As soon as the dough starts to brown it is done. Very carefully remove from the hot pan and serve.

THE CONNOISSEUR

Sandwiches & Wraps

Eat 17 *E9 Burger Bar Bacon Jam Chicken Wrap*

Cheese Posties *Le Bacon Jam Croque Mon Dieu*

Soho Sandwich Company *Bacon Jam & Smoked Mackerel Bagel*

Eat 17 *Bacon Jam & Provolone Quesadilla*

Señor Ceviche *Bacon Jam Chicharonne Sanguche*

In the burger bar at Eat 17 in Hackney, Bacon Jam is an add-on: you can add it to anything. Your choice. Just say the word. It even has its own personalised pink button on the till.

And since we started making Bacon Jam, customers have not been shy at all to do just this. They have added it to anything and everything on the burger bar menu at one time or another, from our pork, blue-cheese, beef or chicken burgers to our halloumi wraps, and even as a side with our triple-fried chips.

One of our favourites, though, is our Bacon Jam Chicken Wrap, so we thought we'd show you how to make it at home. Here's the basic recipe, but the quantities are just a rough guide – make it your own!

1 Make a simple guacamole by mashing the avocado flesh with a fork. Add the lemon juice, tomato and coriander. Season with salt and pepper.

2 Season the chicken breast cubes with salt, pepper and some Cajun seasoning. Fry the seasoned cubes in the olive oil (remember to cook chicken to over 75°C) until cooked through.

3 Place the chicken onto the wrap. Add some Bacon Jam, guacamole, red onion slivers, coleslaw, shredded iceberg lettuce, chipotle sauce and garlic aioli.

4 Roll the wrap tightly. Warm both sides of the wrap in the same pan in which you fried the chicken.

Alternatively …
This wrap is also great with leftover roast chicken. Just shred the chicken and use in place of the cubed breast.

SERVES 1

1 soft avocado, peeled and stoned

a squeeze of lemon juice

1 tomato, finely diced

1 tbsp chopped coriander leaves

sea salt and freshly ground black pepper

160–180g chicken breast, cubed

a sprinkling of Cajun seasoning (we like Old Bay)

olive oil, for frying

38-cm tortilla wrap (durum wheat Turkish wraps work well)

50g Bacon Jam, or to taste

½ red onion, cut into slivers

1 tbsp coleslaw

a handful of shredded iceberg lettuce

1 tsp smoked chipotle sauce

1 tsp garlic aioli

'The transmutation of bacon into condiment form is clearly a huge step forward for mankind. Eat 17 have played a very important role in the part we play of glorifying our customers' lunchtimes. It is with the addition of Bacon Jam that we can safely post the delicious pig that plays such an integral role many of our more eyewateringly delicious sandwich recipes.'

Dave Rotheroe, Cheese Posties

MAKES 2 SANDWICHES

2 eggs

a pinch of sea salt

4 thick slices of corn bread or other good bread

a dash of olive oil

½ avocado, peeled, stoned and sliced

50g goats' cheese, shredded

50g Bacon Jam

'Like Uber, but for grilled cheese' (so says *New York Magazine*), Cheese Posties* post all the ingredients for the perfect cheese toastie directly to your door. Based in Essex, the business was created out of a love for quirky food experiences. Bacon Jam + grilled cheese = a little bit of heaven.

1 Whisk the eggs and salt together in a shallow bowl. Soak the corn bread in the egg mixture on both sides.

2 Heat the oil in a frying pan over a medium-high heat and fry the eggy cornbread for about a minute until nice and brown on both sides.

3 Put the fried bread on a cutting board and load 2 of the slices with sliced avocado and goats' cheese. Smear Bacon Jam thickly on the other 2 slices.

4 Close the sandwiches and return them to the frying pan. Cover and cook over a medium heat for another 3–5 minutes on both sides until the cheese has melted.

IPA
Crate Brewery

(5.8% abv)

More hops and more bite for an intense flavour that stands up well against the richness of all this cheese.

East London Local E17

EAT 17

'It's a delicious sandwich relish. The caramelised onion and smoky bacon flavour is great with the mackerel pâté.'

Dan Silverston, The Soho Sandwich Co.

MAKES 2 BAGELS

1 small cucumber

2 tbsp caster sugar

1 tsp sea salt

3 tbsp rice wine vinegar

300g smoked mackerel, skinned

80g crème fraîche

50g low-fat cream cheese

1 stick celery, finely chopped

juice of ½ lemon

½ tsp grated lemon zest

a twist of freshly ground black pepper

2 sesame seed bagels

handful of salad leaves

90g Bacon Jam

Many of The Soho Sandwich Co.'s* range of more than 100 sandwiches are hand-crafted using ingredients from local suppliers. They supply us with artisan rolls, wraps, paninis and bagels as well as traditional sandwiches.

1 Cut off the ends of the cucumber and cut it in half lengthways, then slice it thinly. Place the slices in a jar.

2 Dissolve the caster sugar and salt in the rice wine vinegar and pour over the cucumber. Pickle them for at least an hour or store in the fridge for up to 3 days.

3 Add half the smoked mackerel to a food processor with the crème fraîche and low-fat cream cheese and blend to a coarse texture. Flake the rest of the mackerel. Stir the blended mackerel/cream cheese mix, chopped celery, lemon juice, lemon zest and black pepper into the flaked mackerel.

4 Slice each bagel. Spread about 3 tablespoons of the mackerel pâté on the bottom half of each bagel, top with 2 pickled cucumber slices, plus some of the crunchy, mixed leaf salad. Spread Bacon Jam on the top slice of each bagel and press the halves together to finish.

*East London Local E2

1 durum wheat wrap

2 tbsp Bacon Jam

a large handful of provolone cheese, grated

1 Spread the wrap generously with Bacon Jam, then sprinkle with grated cheese.

2 Fold the wrap into 4 and cook in a dry pan for 2 minutes each side until the cheese is oozy.

Session IPA
From Three Sods Brewery

(4.4% abv)

Packed full of citrus fruits.

'Can you bring me some more Bacon Jam?
My chefs have eaten both jars – it's that good!'

Harry Edmeades, Señor Ceviche

MAKES 8 SANDWICHES

1 kg pork belly

1½ tbsp sea salt

1½ tbsp ground cumin

1½ tbsp fennel seeds

good-quality hot sauce

105g Bacon Jam

8 soft bread rolls

ice-cold beer, to serve

FOR THE SALSA CRIOLLA

3 red onions, cut into julienne strips

2 tomatoes, deseeded

2 tsp finely chopped coriander leaves

1½ tbsp olive oil

1 tbsp lime juice

Who knew that Bacon Jam deliciousness would make it to Peru? Señor Ceviche* is a Peruvian restaurant and cocktail bar in Carnaby Street in Soho serving street food, super-fresh ceviches and BBQ accompanied by ice-cold Cusqueñas, Mamacitas or anything from the extensive bar menu featuring Peru's much-loved national spirit, Pisco.

1 Preheat the oven to 180°C.

2 Rub the pork belly with 1 tablespoon of the sea salt, most of the cumin and the fennel seeds, and place in a large roasting tin. Cook, uncovered, for 2½ hours until really tender.

3 To make the salsa, mix the red onion, tomatoes and coriander in a bowl. Mix together the olive oil and lime juice and season with the remaining salt and cumin. Use this to dress the salsa.

4 Slice the pork belly into thick strips and coat in the hot sauce to taste (the hotter, the better!).

5 To serve, spread a generous amount of Bacon Jam on the bottom half of each bun, top with 100g of the sliced pork belly, a spoonful of the salsa criolla and the top of the bun. An ice-cold Cusqueña lager is the perfect accompaniment.

London Local W1B

Salad & Eggs

Courtyard Deli *Smoked Tomato & Burrata Salad with Bacon Jam Dressing*

Eat 17 *Bacon Jam, Pear & Squash Salad*

Eat 17 *Pork Belly & Scratchings*

Fenton Eggs *Bacon Jam Baked Eggs*

Treflach Farm *Bacon Jam Scotch Eggs*

Deer Belly *Bacon Jam, Red Onion and Mozzarella Tarts*

102 Courtyard Deli *Smoked Tomato & Burrata Salad with Bacon Jam Dressing*

'This recipe is a bit more effort but smoked tomatoes add a wonderful flavour. Easiest way to make them in your oven is to purchase a Smoker Bag (Amazon sells SAVU Smoker Bags from Finland) and follow the instructions, seasoning your tomatoes with a pinch of salt and sugar before smoking. You can also buy smoked tomatoes from Waitrose or Amazon (use one package) or simply substitute sun-dried tomatoes. This will still provide the umami flavour, just no smokiness.'

Chris Biggers, Courtyard Deli

SERVES 4

105g Bacon Jam

100ml olive oil

200g rocket leaves

2 heads of chicory, separated into leaves

100g radishes, thinly sliced

8 firm, ripe plum tomatoes, cut in half lengthways, seasoned and smoked

4 burrata

1 tsp chopped oregano leaves

Parmesan cheese shavings

1 Place the Bacon Jam in a bowl and add enough oil to loosen it to a dressing consistency. You may not need all the olive oil.

2 Dress the rocket with some of the Bacon Jam dressing and place as the base of the salad in a bowl. Dress the chicory leaves next and add to the bowl, along with the sliced radishes and tomatoes.

3 Ensure the burrata are at room temperature (they will taste far better than straight from the fridge). Place on top of the salad. Scatter over the oregano and dress with the remaining Bacon Jam dressing. Serve topped with lots of shaved Parmesan.

½ butternut squash, peeled and diced

2 tbsp olive oil

1 tsp sea salt

200ml apple cider vinegar

100ml clear honey

2 pears, peeled, cored and chopped

60g Bacon Jam

a few sprigs of flat-leaf parsley, chopped

pork scratchings (see p106 or ready-made), to serve

1 Preheat the oven to 200°C.

2 Toss the squash with the olive oil and salt and spread out in a large roasting tin. Roast in the oven for about 25 minutes until golden.

3 Combine the apple cider vinegar and honey in a small saucepan. Simmer over a medium heat until reduced to a sticky syrup. Set aside to cool.

4 Put the pears into a bowl with the Bacon Jam and mix to coat (or wait and simply dot the jam on each individual salad before serving). Add the squash to the bowl, followed by the vinegar reduction and toss together well.

5 To serve, add some of the pork belly and scratchings (overleaf) to the top of each bowl and sprinkle with parsley.

Neck Oil (Session IPA)
From Beaverton Brewery

(4.3% abv)

Light and crisp. A good complement to the sweetness of fruit

1kg pre-cooked pork belly

Cajun seasoning

oil, for frying new recipe to come

Bacon Jam, to serve

1 Preheat the oven to 220°C.

2 Peel back the skin on the pre-cooked pork belly and scrape away any fat that's left on it. Slice the skin into thin strips and season liberally with Cajun seasoning (Old Bay is great). Place the strips on an oven rack and roast for 15–20 minutes until the skin becomes crackling. Set aside.

3 Dice the pork belly and fry for 1–2 minutes in hot oil until crisp.

4 Serve with Bacon Jam or use in the Pear & Squash Salad on page 104.

Bacon Jam & Beer

Hook Island Red
From The Five Points Brewing Company

(6% abv)

The malty sweetness and aromas of dark plum, bitter cherry and light caramel get a kick from rye malt and American hops.

'I gave these to the family as a starter for lunch yesterday. We were eight in all, ranging in age from 10 to 90, and they were a great success. The Frenchman present gave them 9 out of 10.'

Peggy Hannam, mother-in-law of Andrew Gabriel of Fenton Eggs*

MAKES 4 RAMEKINS

2 tbsp Bacon Jam

4 eggs

4 tbsp double cream

2 rashers of dry-cured streaky bacon

Eat 17's eggs come from a third-generation, small-scale family farm on the Devon/Somerset border that produces award-winning, free-range white, green, brown and blue eggs (from the farm's trademark breed, the Fenton Blue).

1 Preheat the oven to 180°C.

2 Smear about ½ tablespoon of Bacon Jam over the bottom of each of four ramekin dishes. Break one egg on top of each one and spoon a dessertspoon of cream over each egg.

3 Place the ramekins in an ovenproof dish and fill the dish with boiling water so that it comes halfway up the ramekins (a bain marie), then put it in the oven. (Safer yet, pour the boiling water from your kettle into the ovenproof dish after it's already in the oven. What we are trying to avoid is boiling water getting into the ramekins or all over you!) Bake in the oven for 15 minutes for a soft to medium yolk.

4 Meanwhile, fry the bacon or pop it under a hot grill until nice and crisp. Cut or crush into small pieces.

5 Serve the eggs in the ramekins decorated with lots of the bacon bits.

*Eat 17 Supplier

110 Treflach Farm *Bacon Jam Scotch Eggs*

MAKES 4

4 eggs

400g finely minced pork

2 tsp dried sage

2 tsp dried parsley

1 tsp dried marjoram

a grating of fresh nutmeg

½ tsp freshly ground black pepper

a pinch of sea salt

8 tsp Bacon Jam

rapeseed oil, for frying

FOR COATING

flour, for dusting

2 eggs

about 3 tbsp milk

about 100g breadcrumbs

'The Bacon Jam was great for incorporating into the Scotch egg – it really packs a flavour punch, and it's so versatile and easy to work with.'

Lou Kellett, Treflach Farm

On any given day at Eat 17, you'll be sure to find an assortment of free-range meat pies, pasties and sausage rolls from Shropshire's family-run Treflach Farm lining our shelves. Two days a week, they make the 300+ km trip down to London to make sure we are well stocked. Their award-winning Steak & Ale Pie with Stonehouse Brewery ale (which is just down the road from their farm) is a bestseller.

1 Soft-boil the eggs in boiling water for just under 7 minutes for a medium-large egg; any less and they're difficult to peel, any more and you won't get the gooey middle. Plunge them into icy water until cold, then peel and put to one side.

2 Mix the pork with the herbs and spices. Divide into four equal-sized portions. Flatten each portion between two layers of baking paper or freezer bags to a 5mm-thick oval, about 10 x 13cm.

3 Spread 2 tsp of Bacon Jam in the middle of each pork patty, then wrap them carefully around each one of the eggs, gently squeezing as necessary to ensure all the egg is covered and there are no cracks. Dust each Scotch egg in flour.

4 Break the eggs for the coating into a shallow bowl and whisk in enough milk to give it the consistency of thick double cream. Pour the breadcrumbs into a separate shallow bowl. Dip each egg into the egg and milk mixture, then roll in the breadcrumbs. Repeat this process until each egg has been dipped and coated twice.

5 Deep fry the Scotch eggs in hot oil for 9–10 minutes until dark golden brown, or alternatively, swirl the Scotch egg in a little oil in a bowl, then bake in the oven at 180°C for 20–25 minutes. Serve hot or cold.

Alternatively ...

If you'd like your Scotch egg extra spicy or extra crunchy, you can add chilli flakes, oats or some stuffing mix to the breadcrumbs. Substitute Chilli Bacon Jam for even more heat.

'I was surprised how well the Bacon Jam flavour worked. It's a great ingredient to add to baking.'

Joanna Bardzinska, Deer Belly Home Bakery

Homerton-based Deer Belly Home Bakery* have supplied Eat 17 with flapjacks, muffins, slices, granola bars, cakes, loaves and tarts since 2014.

MAKES 6 TARTS

200g plain flour, plus extra for dusting

a pinch of sea salt

75g butter, chilled and diced

50g + 6 tbsp mozzarella cheese, grated

3 eggs

150ml double cream

100g natural yogurt

sea salt and freshly ground black pepper

105g Bacon Jam

1 Sift flour and salt into a large bowl. Add the butter and rub it into the flour with your fingertips until the mixture resembles breadcrumbs. Add the 50g of mozzarella and stir until the cheese is just mixed in. Pour in 1 beaten egg and mix just enough to bring the pastry together.

2 Transfer to lightly floured worktop and knead until smooth but try not to handle the dough too much. Wrap in cling film and leave to chill in the fridge for 30 minutes.

3 Grease a six-hole tart tin.

4 On the lightly floured worktop, roll out the pastry to about 2mm thick. Cut out six 15cm circles and line your tart tin with them, pricking each base with a fork. Leave to chill in the fridge for 30 minutes.

5 Meanwhile, preheat the oven to 200°C.

6 Insert paper baking cases over the top of your tart pastry and fill with baking beans. Bake in the oven for 10 minutes. Remove the paper cases and beans and return the pastry to the oven for 5 minutes.

7 Reduce the oven temperature to 180°C.

8 Whisk the 2 remaining eggs with the cream, yogurt and salt and pepper. Put aside. Spread 2 tablespoons of Bacon Jam over each pastry base. Fill the pastry cases evenly with the egg mixture. Sprinkle 1 tablespoon of grated mozzarella on top of each tart. Bake for 20 minutes or until the filling has just set. Leave to cool for 10 minutes before serving.

*Supplier and East London Local E9

BRANG HOME THAT
Bacon

Pasta & Gnocchi

Eat 17 *Sweetcorn & Bacon Jam Gnocchi*

Hank's Po' Boys *Bacon Jam Smoky
Mac 'n' Cheese*

The Fresh Pasta Company *Bacon Jam
Mascarpone Mezzalune*

Hack & Veldt Delicatessen
Meaty Bacon Jam Pasta Sauce

116 Eat 17 Sweetcorn & Bacon Jam Gnocchi

SERVES 2

½ butternut squash, peeled, seeded and diced

75ml whole milk

75ml single cream

2 tbsp olive oil

½ red onion, finely sliced

1 garlic clove, crushed

2 sprigs of thyme, leaves chopped

2 cobs sweetcorn (vac-packed is okay)

a knob of butter

200g gnocchi

150g chestnut mushrooms, chopped

½ red onion, diced

a generous splash of white wine

105g Bacon Jam

sea salt and freshly ground black pepper

3 chives, chopped

1 Cook the squash in a saucepan of boiling water for about 10 minutes until tender, then drain. Put the squash into a food processor or blender with the milk and cream and season with salt. Purée until you have a double cream-like consistency.

2 Heat a dash of olive oil and slow-cook the finely sliced onion for about 15 minutes over a low heat with the garlic and thyme leaves.

3 Grill the cobs evenly under a hot grill to give them a nice colour but be careful they don't burn. When they're charred, cut off the kernels.

4 Heat a heavy-bottomed saucepan and add the butter and remaining oil. When the butter is beginning to colour, pop in your gnocchi, mushrooms and diced onion and allow to brown for 2–3 minutes. Add the wine and boil over a high heat to reduce for a minute.

5 Reduce to a lower heat. Add the corn, squash purée, Bacon Jam and slow-cooked onions to the pan and warm through for 1–2 minutes, stirring occasionally. Season with salt and pepper to taste. Serve sprinkled with the chives.

Leap Year Golden Ale
From Three Sods Brewery

(5.0% abv)

A hearty meal requires a hearty beer. Sweet malts balanced with slight tropical fruit flavours.

'We developed this stove-top version of a southern-style mac 'n' cheese to prepare from our street food cart, but it works just as well at home for a quick and easy comfort food hit.'

Victoria Thake, Hank's Po' Boys

Weekdays at KERB lunchtime markets and every weekend at the Southbank Centre, Simon Drake and Victoria Thake offer their take on Cajun, Creole and Southern cuisine. They started Hank's* in 2014 in Deptford, south-east London, after a last-minute trip to New Orleans, Louisiana, where they fell in love with the city. They've been using Bacon Jam on their Smoky Mac 'n' Cheese since 2014.

SERVES 4

500g dry macaroni
(large tubes, preferably)

50g butter

65g plain flour

½ tsp sea salt

½ heaped tsp mustard powder

¼ tsp freshly ground black pepper

¼ tsp smoked paprika, plus extra for dusting

600ml semi-skimmed milk

150g smoked Cheddar cheese, grated

150g mature Cheddar cheese, grated

good-quality hot sauce, to taste

4 tbsp Bacon Jam

1 Cook the macaroni in boiling salted water, according to the packet instructions, until al dente. Drain and rinse in cold water to stop the cooking process (if the macaroni is too soft it will break up when added to the cheese sauce later).

2 In a heavy-based pan, melt the butter, then add the flour, salt, mustard powder, pepper and smoked paprika, stirring constantly for 3 minutes. Add the milk and whisk over a low heat for 10 minutes until the sauce thickens.

3 Remove from the heat and gently stir in two-thirds of the grated cheeses a handful at a time until fully melted. Return the pan to a low heat then add the macaroni and stir everything together for 3–4 minutes to heat the pasta through.

4 Spoon the macaroni into serving bowls, sprinkle the remaining cheese over the top of each bowl. If you have a chef's blowtorch melt the cheese until nicely browned. Alternatively if your bowls are heatproof, you can place them under a pre-heated grill for 30 seconds.

5 Add a generous splash of hot sauce and top each bowl with a spoonful of Bacon Jam. Stir through before eating.

Alternatively ...
This is also great with a handful of crayfish tails, a light dusting of smoked paprika and a pinch of cayenne pepper stirred through at the end.

*Bacon Jam Stockist & London Local SE1

120 The Fresh Pasta Company *Bacon Jam Mascarpone Mezzalune*

SERVES 4

2 tbsp finely chopped rosemary leaves,

300g mascarpone cheese

sea salt and freshly ground black pepper

500g '00' wheat flour, plus extra for dusting

4 large eggs

2 egg yolks

105g Bacon Jam

melted butter and freshly grated Parmesan cheese, to serve

'Not quite a traditional Italian recipe but definitely a memorable one, with its sweet, savoury and smoky flavour topped by the luxurious texture of mascarpone and enhanced with a twist of rosemary.'
Sole Nasi, The Fresh Pasta Company

Restaurant-quality fresh pasta created since 2004 near Verona in Northern Italy with premium ingredients like black truffle, venison, Buffalo milk ricotta and Barolo wine. For tips and tricks on making fresh pasta painlessly, take a look at thefreshpastacompany.com.

1 Mix the rosemary into the mascarpone. Season to taste with salt and pepper and chill in the fridge until needed, bringing it to room temperature before using.

2 Make a mound of the flour on a wooden board or work surface and create a well in the centre. Crack in 3 of the eggs and both the yolks. Sprinkle in some salt. Break the egg yolks with the fingertips of one hand and incorporate them into the flour with a circular motion until you have worked it enough to start bringing it all together into a ball. Knead the dough for 10–15 minutes until smooth.

3 Cover the pasta ball with two layers of cling film to prevent it from drying out, and leave to rest for 1 hour. The dough can be made a day ahead, wrapped and refrigerated and brought to room temperature before proceeding.

4 Roll the dough through a pasta machine. Pass the dough through the machine 3 times, starting with widest setting and finishing your last pass on the finest, folding it before each new pass through the machine until it is about 1.5mm thick. The pasta should be nice and shiny.

5 Lay the pasta strip on a flour-dusted work surface and cut into 9cm circles with a round cutter. Fill the centre of each circle with ½ teaspoon rosemary mascarpone and ½ teaspoon Bacon Jam.

6 Beat the remaining egg. Brush the perimeter of each circle with beaten egg, then carefully lift one side of the circle and fold it over the filling to the other side, enclosing

the filling. Press to seal the parcel, making sure you press out any air around the filling. Use a fork to decorate and seal each half-moon.

7 Cook the mezzalune in plenty of slowly boiling salted water for about 3–4 minutes, then drain well.

8 Serve hot with melted butter and freshly grated Parmesan cheese.

122 Hack & Veldt Delicatessen
Meaty Bacon Jam Pasta Sauce

'The Bacon Jam gives a much richer depth of flavour than even a nice bit of smoked pancetta ever could. If you like your spice, use the Chilli Bacon Jam. If you prefer an even richer paprika-tinged hint, go for Chorizo Jam.'

Maike Hachfeld, Hack & Veldt Delicatessen

SERVES 4

a knob of butter

a dash of olive oil

1 carrot, finely diced

1 onion, finely diced

2 celery sticks, finely diced

105g Bacon Jam

150g tomato purée

250g coarsely minced beef, at room temperature

250g coarsely minced pork, at room temperature

sea salt and white pepper

150ml whole milk

150ml dry white wine

400ml tin of plum tomatoes

a dash of Worcestershire sauce

a sprinkling of dried oregano

a pinch of sugar

spaghetti or penne and grated Parmesan cheese, to serve

In the heart of Chiswick on Turnham Green Terrace, independent Hack & Veldt Delicatessen* opened in 2012. Maike says she only sells things she loves so we're very happy that she stocks our Bacon Jam.

1 Melt the butter and oil in a large, heavy-based frying pan set over a gentle heat. Add the carrot, onion and celery and cook until softened. Add the Bacon Jam and cook for 5 minutes, then add the tomato purée and cook for a further 2 minutes.

2 Crumble the beef and pork into the pan and brown, stirring occasionally to break up any lumps. Season generously with salt and white pepper. Stir in the milk and let simmer gently until almost all the milk has evaporated, which should take about 30 minutes.

3 Add the wine and the tomatoes and stir well. Add the Worcestershire sauce, oregano and a pinch of sugar to sweeten the tomatoes. Put a lid on the pan, and cook for at least 1 hour (2 is even better) until the meat is very tender. Check on the sauce occasionally. Don't let it go dry.

4 Serve with spaghetti or penne and lots of grated Parmesan cheese.

*Bacon Jam Stockist & London Local W4

Beans & Veggies

Eat 17 *Bacon Jam Baked Beans*

Eat 17 *Toasted Bacon Jam Crumbs*

Ginger's Kitchen *Bacon Jam Butterbean Soup*

Wildes Cheese *Cheesy Roast Bacon Jam Cauliflower*

Eat 17 *Bacon Jam Candied Collard Greens*

Wildes Cheese *Roast Squash & Bacon Jam Pesto*

SERVES 4

1 onion, diced

a knob of butter

a dash of olive oil

2 garlic cloves, minced

½ tsp fennel seeds

½ tsp cayenne pepper

½ tsp smoked paprika

200ml passata

2 tsp brown sugar

1 tsp balsamic vinegar

400g cooked cannellini
beans, drained and rinsed

2 tbsp Bacon Jam

sea salt and freshly ground
black pepper

EAT 17 TOASTED BACON JAM
CRUMBS

3 pieces of bread or brioche
buns, diced

olive oil

60g Bacon Jam

1 Sweat the onion in the butter and olive oil over a medium heat until softened. Add the garlic and all the spices and cook for a further 2 minutes.

2 Add the passata, sugar and vinegar, bring to the boil, then simmer for 30 minutes, stirring every 5 minutes or so, until the sauce has reduced by about one-fifth.

3 Coat the beans in the Bacon Jam, then add to the pan and cook for a further 15 minutes. Season with salt and pepper. Serve with some crispy onions or toasted Bacon Jam crumbs.

Eat 17 *Toasted Bacon Jam Crumbs*

'To add a little Bacon Jam crunch to anything you make.'
Chris, Eat 17

1 Preheat the oven to 160°C.

2 Put the buns in a bowl with the Bacon Jam and pour in a generous amount of olive oil. Massage the mix thoroughly with your hands until the bread is completely saturated with the oil and jam.

3 Spread the cubes evenly on a baking sheet and bake for about 15 minutes, making sure they don't burn. Leave to cool. Crush the cubes with your hands to make crumbs or put them in a plastic bag and crush with a rolling pin. Use immediately or keep on hand for later.

*'I had found some Spanish recipes with bacon
and thought the jam would really sweeten up
nicely against the smoked paprika.'*

Dave Cook, Ginger's Kitchen

SERVES 4

1 medium white onion, diced

1½ tbsp rapeseed oil

2 tsp garlic, chopped

1 celery stick, diced

1 carrot, diced

1 tbsp tomato purée

5 tbsp tinned butterbeans,
drained

400ml chicken stock

2 tbsp chunks of roasted
red peppers

400g tinned chopped
tomatoes

1 tsp smoked paprika
(sweet or hot)

a pinch thyme leaves

2 tbsp Bacon Jam

sea salt and freshly ground
black pepper

habas fritas and finely sliced
red onion with parsley, to
serve

West Sussex-based Ginger's Kitchen* has been
supplying Walthamstow and Hackney since 2014
with chef prepared meals including their Great Taste
Award-winning Florentine Fish Pie (made with Wild
Alaskan salmon and sustainably sourced smoked
coley), their nut-free Pesto Pasta Salad and their
warm and zingy Thai Chicken Curry.

1 In a heavy-based saucepan, soften the onions in the
rapeseed oil. Add the garlic, celery and carrots and fry until
lightly coloured. Add the tomato purée and stir well.

2 Pour the butterbeans, chicken stock, roasted pepper
chunks, tomatoes, smoked paprika and thyme into the pan.
Cook for 30–40 minutes until the carrots are soft but not
completely cooked. Add the Bacon Jam and simmer for
5 minutes.

3 Cool the soup a little, then transfer to a food processor.
Blend until fairly smooth but try to leave a little bit of
texture. Season with salt and pepper to taste.

4 Scatter with salted habas fritas and serve with finely
sliced red onion mixed with chopped parsley.

Alternatively ...
This calls for Bacon Jam but in fact it's even better with
Chorizo Jam.

*Eat 17 Supplier

'Alexandra, AKA Ally Pally White, is a semi-hard artisan handmade cheese originally named after Alexandra Palace.'

Keith Sides, Wildes Cheese

SERVES 4

3 garlic cloves, chopped

4 spring onions, finely chopped

1 tsp smoked paprika

a squeeze of lemon or lime juice

2 tsp Bacon Jam

a handful of chopped coriander

2 tbsp extra virgin olive oil

sea salt and freshly ground black pepper

1 large cauliflower

300g cherry tomatoes, halved

100g Alexandra cheese, grated (good substitutes are Caerphilly or a rich creamy Cheddar (any nutty, buttery cheese with a good melt))

From out of Tottenham, North London comes award-winning urban artisan cheese maker, Wildes Cheese*, supplying Eat 17 with their own-recipe cheeses using milk from a single herd of cows located just outside Rye in East Sussex. Started in 2012, they also offer cheese-making courses to the public.

1 Preheat the oven to 200°C.

2 In a bowl, mix the garlic, spring onions, smoked paprika, lemon juice, Bacon Jam and coriander. Loosen with olive oil and season with salt and pepper. Trim the outer cauliflower leaves, remove the stalk to the base of the cauliflower and scoop or cut out the hard core of the remaining stalk.

3 Rub the Bacon Jam mix over the whole cauliflower, then put it into an ovenproof casserole dish with a lid. Place the halved cherry tomatoes around the base of the cauliflower and drizzle them with a little olive oil. Cover and cook for 1 hour until tender.

4 Scatter the grated cheese over the cauliflower and return it to the oven, uncovered, for 5 minutes, or until the cheese has melted.

Eat 17 Suplier & London Local N17

16 leaves of collard greens

50g Bacon Jam

2 red onions, thinly sliced

4 streaky bacon rashers, cut into strips

2 tsp sugar

2 tsp sea salt

Bacon Jam Crumbs (see page 127)

1 Blanch the collard greens in boiling water for 1 minute until slightly softened, then drain. When cool enough to handle, core the leaves and cut into long ribbons about 1.5cm wide. Add the Bacon Jam to the ribbons and toss to coat.

2 Fry the onions and bacon together in a large saucepan with sugar and salt, stirring, until the mixture caramelises. Add the collard green ribbons and stir to combine. Cook until the greens are tender, about 2 or 3 minutes.

3 Serve with a crunchy topping of Bacon Jam crumbs.

Bacon Jam & Beer

Stout

From Crate Brewery

(5.7% abv)

A lush combination of sweet and savoury notes with dark forest fruits and roasted coffee.

'High Cross is a white crumbly cheese that has been lightly brined and is a little salty.'

Keith Sides, Wildes Cheese

SERVES 4

1 large butternut squash, peeled, seeded and cut into chunks

a drizzle of olive oil

sea salt and freshly ground black pepper

2 tsp Bacon Jam

1 tsp smoked or sweet paprika

2 garlic cloves

1 large bunch of coriander

50g walnuts

120g High Cross cheese, cut into small dice (good substitutes are feta or Cheshire cheese)

100ml extra virgin olive oil

juice of ½ lime

green salad and crusty bread, to serve

For this recipe, Wildes use High Cross cheese which is similar in texture to Wensleydale, but you can substitute feta or Cheshire cheese if neither of these are available.

1 Preheat the oven to 200°C.

2 Put the butternut squash in a bowl, drizzle with olive oil, season with salt and pepper and toss until coated. Spread evenly over a baking sheet and roast in the oven for about 40 minutes or until the squash is lightly browned and tender.

3 Put the Bacon Jam, paprika, garlic, coriander and walnuts into a food processer and pulse until it makes a paste. Save a little of the cheese for garnish and add the rest to the processor with half the extra virgin olive oil and pulse until the pesto is loose. Then add the remaining oil and the lime juice and season with salt and pepper.

4 To serve, spoon the pesto over the squash and lightly stir in, garnishing with the remaining cheese. Accompany this with salad leaves and crusty bread. If you have pesto left over, place in a jar, cover with olive oil and keep in the fridge for up to a week.

Sweets

Cutter & Squidge *Bacon Jam Blueberry S'mores*

Pearl & Groove *Bacon Jam Brownies*

Vicky's Donuts *Maple Bacon Jam Donut*

'The savoury thyme flavour of the Bacon Jam works a treat with the marshmallow, white chocolate, house-made blueberry jam and maple.'

Annabel Lui, Cutter & Squidge*

MAKES 12

100g wholemeal flour

100g plain flour

50g light soft brown sugar

½ tsp sea salt

100g butter

2 tbsp maple syrup

TO SERVE

Bacon Jam

salted pretzels

blueberry jam

square of white chocolate

maple syrup

marshmallows

In Soho, Annabel Lui and her sister Emily run an all-natural bakery specialising in biscuits, cookies, cakes and their own signature 'Biskie', a combination of all three.

1 Preheat the oven to 180°C.

2 Mix the flours, brown sugar and salt. Melt the butter and add it to the dry ingredients. Add the maple syrup. Either in a mixer or by hand, bring all the ingredients together into a dough. Roll out into a 2mm thick, 10cm x 10cm sheet, cut into 24 squares and place on baking sheet. Bake for 10–15 minutes until golden brown. Allow to cool.

3 On one cracker, spread a nice bit of Bacon Jam and stick a salty pretzel on top of it. On the other cracker, spread some blueberry jam, put a square of white chocolate on top of it and drizzle over a little maple syrup.

4 Toast the marshmallow on a sharp stick over an open campfire. If you are not camping, use a blowtorch or try the flame on your gas stovetop. The important thing is just to get the marshmallow brown and roasty and gooey (don't let it catch on fire, though).

5 Now slide your gooey, toasted marshmallow off your sharp stick (or skewer or fork) and onto the bacon-jam/pretzel covered cracker and squish the other, blueberry jam/chocolate-covered half of the cracker on top to make a sweet, succulent sandwich. Repeat until you have used all the crackers.

*London Local W1F

'Cut into squares and spoon a dollop of maple ice cream, sprinkles of crispy bacon and some chilli flakes on top. For even more heat, substitute Chilli Bacon Jam.'

Serena Whitefield, Pearl & Groove

MAKES 16

350g dark chocolate

250g unsalted butter, plus extra for greasing

50g ground almonds

1 tsp baking powder

3 free-range eggs

250g light soft brown sugar

1 tbsp Bacon Jam

maple syrup ice cream, crispy bacon and chilli flakes, to serve

Pearl & Groove,* the flourless bakery, opened in 2013. The photos under CAKE PORN on the P&G website might make you want to eat nothing but cake all day every day but... relax! Each one is gluten free, and many are sugar and dairy free too. And now all their dreams have come true with the opening of their beautiful new shop on Portobello Road in London. They deliver their gluten-free goodies to Eat 17 three times a week.

1 Preheat the oven to 170°C and lightly grease a 20cm square baking tin.

2 Melt the chocolate and butter very gently over a low heat. Set aside and allow to cool slightly.

3 Combine the almonds and baking powder, gently breaking up any lumps with a small whisk or fork.

4 Whisk the eggs until thick and creamy. Gradually add the sugar until the consistency is really thick and mousse-like.

5 Fold the egg mixture into the cooled chocolate a little at a time, alternating with Bacon Jam and almonds until everything is incorporated.

6 Spoon mixture into the prepared tin and bake for 40–45 minutes. Leave to cool in the tin.

*Eat Supplier & London Local W10

'Sometimes (and always when hungover), only a breakfast of sugar and bacon will do. This donut is a perfect combination of salt and sweet, and is a great twist on the bacon sandwich.'

Vicky Graham, Vicky's Donuts

MAKES 6

250g strong white bread flour, plus extra for dusting

20g sugar

25g butter

5g sea salt

6g dried yeast

1 free-range egg

80ml whole milk, warm

55ml water

1.5 litres vegetable oil

100g icing sugar, sifted

1 tbsp dark maple syrup

½ tbsp boiling water

2 tbsp Bacon Jam

12 good-quality streaky bacon rashers

Vicky set up Vicky's Donuts* in 2015, and then promptly won a *BBC Good Food Bursary Award*. To celebrate, she and her team make handmade donuts in their kitchen in Dalston, and sell them online and at Chatsworth Road Market.

1 Place the flour, sugar and butter in a large bowl. Make two wells in the flour at opposite sides of the bowl and add the salt to one, and the yeast to the other. Break in the eggs and add the warmed milk. Measure out the water to have it ready at your side.

2 If you're using a stand mixer, attach the dough hook and mix on the slowest speed setting while slowly pouring the water into the dough mixture. If you don't have a stand mixer, use one hand to bring the dough together and the other to add the water. Once all the water has been added and all the ingredients have been incorporated, you'll have a sticky, wet mixture.

3 Knead in the mixer on a slow setting for 8 minutes or on a floured surface using your hands for 10 minutes. When it's been kneaded enough, it'll be smooth, elastic and have a shiny surface. Put the dough in a clean bowl and cover with a damp tea towel for 1 hour. Grease 2 oven trays with a tablespoon of the vegetable oil.

4 Cover your hands with flour and sprinkle a flat surface with it too. Tip out the dough and knead with your hands a little to form a ball. Sprinkle the rolling pin with flour and roll out the dough to about 2cm thick. Use a round-donut cutter with a hole in the middle to cut out ring shapes and place these onto the greased trays. Knead any leftover dough and roll out to repeat the process until you end up with 12 rings. Leave to rise for 30 minutes.

*East London Local E9

5 Preheat a deep-fat fryer or, using a thermometer, bring the oil in a heavy-based pan to 180°C. Use a fish slice to carefully pick up each round of dough and put it into the fryer or pan (2–3 at a time, if you want), cooking each one for around 60 seconds on both sides or until golden brown. Remove the cooked donuts from the oil with tongs and place onto a baking tray lined with a paper towel to soak up any excess oil. Leave to cool.

6 Mix the icing sugar, maple syrup and boiling water together and put to one side. Fry the bacon rashers on a medium heat in a little oil in a frying pan until crisp.

7 Using a bread knife, slice the cool donuts horizontally, as if cutting a bagel, and spread about ½ tsp of Bacon Jam onto each side.

8 To serve, place 2 rashers of bacon inside each donut sandwich and finish with a drizzle of maple glaze and a rasher of crispy bacon on top.

Knitted bacon

Moles and Voles Love BACON ROLLS

EAT 17

OVEN TEMPERATURES

°C	Fan °C	°F	Gas	Description
110	90	225	¼	Very cool
120	100	250	½	Very cool
140	120	275	1	Cool
150	130	300	2	Cool
160	140	325	3	Warm
180	160	350	4	Moderate
190	170	375	5	Moderately hot
200	180	400	6	Fairly hot
220	200	425	7	Hot
230	210	450	8	Very hot
240	220	475	8	Very hot

WEIGHTS FOR DRY INGREDIENTS

Metric	Imperial	Metric	Imperial	Metric	Imperial
7g	¼ oz	225g	8oz	750g	1lb 11oz
15g	½ oz	250g	9oz	800g	1¾lb
20g	¾ oz	275g	10oz	900g	2lb
25g	1 oz	300g	11oz	1kg	2¼lb
40g	1 oz	350g	12oz	1.1kg	2½lb
50g	2oz	375g	13oz	1.25kg	2¾lb
60g	2 oz	400g	14oz	1.35kg	3lb
75g	3oz	425g	15oz	1.5kg	3lb 6oz
100g	3 oz	450g	1lb	1.8kg	4lb
125g	4oz	500g	1lb 2oz	2kg	4½lb
140g	4 oz	550g	1¼lb	2.25kg	5lb
150g	5oz	600g	1lb 5oz	2.5kg	5½lb
165g	5 oz	650g	1lb 7oz	2.75kg	6lb
175g	6oz	675g	1½lb		
200g	7oz	700g	1lb 9oz		

BACON
— is like a —
HIGH-FIVE
FOR MY MOUTH.

LIQUID MEASURES

Metric	Imperial	Aus	US
25ml	1fl oz		
50ml	2fl oz	¼ cup	¼ cup
75ml	3fl oz		
100ml	3 fl oz		
120ml	4fl oz	½ cup	½ cup
150ml	5fl oz		
175ml	6fl oz	¾ cup	¾ cup
200ml	7fl oz		
250ml	8fl oz	1 cup	1 cup
300ml	10fl oz/½ pint	½ pint	1¼ cups
360ml	12fl oz		
400ml	14fl oz		
450ml	15fl oz	2 cups	2½ cups/1 pint
600ml	1 pint	1 pint	2 cups
750ml	1¼ pints		
900ml	1½ pints		
1 litre	1¾ pints	1¾ pints	1 quart
1.2 litres	2 pints		
1.4 litres	2½ pints		
1.5 litres	2½ pints		
1.7 litres	3 pints		
2 litres	3½ pints		
3 litres	5¼ pints		

UK-AUSTRALIAN TABLESPOON CONVERSIONS

1 x UK or Australian teaspoon is 5ml

1 x UK tablespoon is 3 teaspoons/15ml

1 Australian tablespoon is 4 teaspoons/20ml

Acknowledgements

Art & Artists

Jamie Reed @ Human Shaped Robot
(page iv) *Eat BBQ*, (page 38) *The Folsom*, (page 88) *The Connoisseur*, (page 114) *Brang Home That Bacon* © Jamie Reed @ Human Shaped Robot (www.humanshapedrobot.com).

Robert Kurtz
(page vii) *Lenka & Liz DD DO Bacon* © Robert Kurtz (www.dotnethed.com).

Dan Goodsell
(page viii) *We Could Sizzle Together* (featuring Shaky Bacon) © Dan Goodsell (www.MisterToast.com).

Sara Robbins-Page @ Heavenstobessie
(page 9)'*I Love You Like Grilled Cheese and Bacon*' necklace © Sara Robbins-Page @ heavenstobessie (www.etsy.com/shop/heavenstobessie).

Caanan Grall
(page 10) *Bacon is What?!* © Caanan Grall (www.occasionalcomics.com).

Elli Luca Designs
(page 11) *Pug Bacon Love*, (page 76) *Pug Stealing Bacon* © Elli Luca (www.elliluca.com; www.etsy.com/shop/ElliLucaDesigns).

Alexis Trice @ Welcome To The Doghouse
(pages 16–17) *Catching Some Bacon Waves* © Alexis Trice @ Welcome To The Doghouse (www.welcometothedoghouse.net; www.alexistrice.com).

Tasja Sachs
(pages 26–27) *Bacon Baby* © Tasja Sachs (www.etsy.com/shop/TasjCollage).

Jean Jullien
(page 54) *Eat 17 Bacon Jam Jar* © Jean Jullien (www.jeanjullien.com).

Allyson Gutchell @ Turddemon
(page 66) *Boston Terrier Bacon* © Allyson Gutchell @ Turddemon (www.etsy.com/shop/turddemon).

George Otsubo
(endpaper & page 100) *Magic Bacon Ride* © George Otsubo (www.georgeotsubo.com; www.threadless.com).

Jesse Azarian @ Star Trek and Bacon

(page 136) *Fascinating* © Jesse Azarian @ Star Trek and Bacon (www.etsy.com/shop/startrekandbacon).

James Ward @ Jimbobart

(page 145) *Moles and Voles Love Bacon Rolls* © James Ward @ Jimbobart (www.jimbobart.com).

Tara Acheson @ HEARTprintshop

(page 109) *We Belong Together* © Tara Acheson @ HEARTprintshop (www.etsy.com/shop/HEARTprintshop).

Melissa Gable

(page 124) *Bacon and Eggs Couture* © Melissa Gable (www.onecreativegirl.com).

Photography

(pages 6 & 7) Jamie Dodd @ Jamie Dodd Photography (www.jamiedoddphotography.co.uk).

(page 8) Meat Porn UK (meatpornuk.com).

(page 12) Etienne Gilfillan (instagram.com/etiennephotography).

Food

(pages 30, 36, 41, 46, 48, 52, 56, 60, 62, 64, 78, 80, 96, 104, 106, 112, 116 and 126) Rosie Edwards.

(pages 34, 42, 44, 59, 83, 84, 94, 128, 130, 134 and 138) Kyle Nimmo (www.nimmocreative.com).

(page 68) Etienne Gilfillan (instagram.com/etiennephotography).

(page 71) David Hoffman (www.hoffmanphotos.com).

(page 121) Simona Carini (www.simonacarini.com)

(pages 50 and 74) Nick Warner (www.nickwarner.co.uk) & stylist Eloise James (www.eloisejames.co.uk).

(pages 18–22) The Instagrams appear courtesy of Eat 17 customers.

All other food photos courtesy of Eat 17 contributors.

Bacon Miscellany

(page vi) *Bacon Beans*, (page 2) *Gummy Bacon* and (page 144) *Bacon Wool* courtesy of The Kate Hibbert Bacornucopia (thanks to Dan Mallory, Beth Tessier and Liam Payne respectively).

(page vii) *Bacon Inhaler* courtesy of firebox.co.uk.

(page 28) *Sex, Drugs & Bacon Rolls* neon at The Breakfast Club in Spitalfields, London (www.thebreakfastclubcafes.com).

(page 49) *Reclining Bacon* courtesy of Save On Meats, East Hastings, Vancouver, Canada.

(page 103) *Either You Love Bacon...* photo courtesy of Pam Morris.

(page 147) 24 Hour Tees (www.24hrtees.net/).

(page 151) Russell Darling (www.flickr.com/photos/russelldarling/albums).

Recipes

All recipes © the original creators.

Models

(page 90) Special thanks to Danny from Eat 17 Models.